Professional Freedom In the Midst of Chaos

Marilyn Carroll, PhD

ISBN:098370340X
ISBN-13:0983703402

What an excellent book! My whole career has centered on doing the things that are my passion as opposed to the 'job' or 'field' that I trained for. I have worked in multiple industries, multiple roles and multiple functions within companies, but in every case I focus on some type of business transformation or performance improvement, and building and executing operational strategies. The coolest thing is that now I've started mentoring the next generation of young career women - something I did not have. That is why your book will be so powerful.

"A powerful book that gives us the toolkit for career advancement in our age - global, knowledge focused, socially inter-connected and instantaneous. Marilyn reminds us that staying true to our passion helps us navigate through that paradigm shift and succeed in all parts of our lives."

Marilyn Jentzen, Vice President, Operations Center Strategy Global Growth and Operations, Thomson Reuters

"Dr. Carroll has captured the concepts of career management for the 21st century in her book "Professional Freedom in the Midst of Chaos". How timely as the world of work is rapidly changing, requiring professionals to take charge of their personal lives and careers in a methodical, focused and adaptable manner. This guide is invaluable for those whose careers have changed, are changing, or will change…meaningful for everyone as we adjust to the transformational workplace"

Jennifer L. Scully, President and CEO Clinical Resources, LLC

"I've read endless professional development books that offer temporary motivation; and lack direction on career strategy. Professional Freedom is a breath of fresh air, a literal roadmap to professional success. It requires us to be deliberate in our career advancement efforts."

Katrina Taylor, CEO

"In Professional Freedom in the Midst of Chaos Dr. Carroll has extracted the critical factors to take control of professional and personal decisions. This book serves as a roadmap for career management."

Rita Izaguirre, J.D., SPHR (Former head of Talent Acquisition at SunTrust Banks)

"This book serves the underemployed, the overworked, the unemployed, and the entrepreneur. By knowing you personally I know you have lived this book, which is why people always want to know how you do what you do."

President, Taylor Legacy Group

DEDICATION

This book is dedicated to my family, friends, students, and those experiencing a paradigm shift in their career and life. I pray that this work helps you to achieve your goals by providing you with the solutions used by others and myself on how we reinvented ourselves along our own paths in life to achieve our desired levels of success.

"We have different gifts; according to the grace given us. If a man's gift is prophesying, let him use it in proportion to his faith. If it is serving, let him serve; if it is encouraging, let him encourage; if it is contributing to the needs of others, let him give generously; if it is leadership, let him govern diligently; if it is showing mercy, let him do it cheerfully." The One Year Bible: The New International Version (1996).

Professional Freedom

I am free and happy because I know who I am and I understand the big picture.

I understand the quality of life I want and seek.

I have a value system which allows me to stay within my ethical boundaries.

I am free and happy because I am prepared for the world of opportunities presented before me and I know what my profession means to me and I to it; remaining knowledgeable about what makes my craft work.

I understand how to build what I seek, my foundation is strong, my connections are getting stronger, and my giving is strong.

The use of my talents is displayed in everything I do.

My image is strong and my ability to connect with others to achieve a common goal is stronger.

My vision of the future strengthens me and those around me.

My ability to dream, understand, achieve, build, rebuild, and test the waters time after time have lead me to an eye, mind and heart for the big picture.

I am free and happy because I understand and have positioned myself to play a starting role in the big picture.

I move each day towards self-actualization through paths of behaviors and the wealth of knowledge I now have within me.

I am free and happy because each day I awake to a world encompassing the right feelings, emotions, allure and satisfaction I receive in knowing that I am professionally free.

This is me!

CONTENTS

ACKNOWLEDGMENTS

I would like to thank the two groups who went through the twelve week training program which was the bases for this book. Many of you came out on Saturdays or Wednesdays to go through the program. I thank you for your valuable feedback.

I would also like to thank Amy Dixon for reading , editing and providing suggestions to me. You were great! I wish you the best on your new editing company.

Thanks also to the pro athletes who join me on my radio show to discuss many of the variables outlined in this book. Please know that I truly appreciated your valuable time, expertise, and efforts.

Finally, I would like to thank all my friends, ex- teammates, and students who supported me through their words of encouragement and support in completing tasks which helped me to achieve my goals. You guys are the best.

INTRODUCTION

Rules of the Game

Do you wonder why some people can sustain economic positioning while others can't? Do you think that career success is luck or the universe lining up behind an individual's success? Do you think the type of company or manager you work for impacts your career success? Maybe you think that some people's career success was meant to be therefore they have it. Well, the only way to true career success is preparation. That preparation involves several key areas including: what you know, who you know, power of influence, knowledge of who you are, level of career market knowledge, skills and abilities, changeability, how others see you, community connectivity, financial responsibility, and your goals. We all have a purpose in life. Therefore, we are all here to serve some good.

Over the last five years I have examine why some people master career success while others don't. In my role as a manager/leader, I often witness individuals with talents but lacking other key attributes that contribute towards success. At every level of our career various success determining components as outlined in this book are needed in order to keep moving on to new career paradigms.

In this writing we classify career paradigms as transactional, technical, and tactical. Just as we are continuous in shaping and growing, so must our career strategy. Our actions at the entry level, transactional will not be the same to gain technical or tactical entry. How we prepare and respond to the components of the economic environment, as it relates to our career, will impact our ability to grow and maintain career sustainability.

Each career tier or paradigm requires change to remain competitive. For example, levels of knowledge, skill, ability, and education are high at transactional levels. However, at the technical level the same four are still required at an enhanced level. Political, social, and psychological aspects are required and must be demonstrated through our official marketing/branding, or how others see us.

The last level, tactical, is a blend of technical but with more of a focus on political, social, psychological and branding. An example is the level of influence needed at the transactional level is low. However, in order to stay in the game, the influence level must increase as we move up to the next levels. Influence is paramount at the tactical levels. It is important to understand that at the base of each paradigm is foundational knowledge which is built through experience, assessments and goals.

By the same token being prepared is inclusive of our knowledge of the impact of technology on current and future career paradigms. The universe is based on cause and effect. Every major technology shift has a cause and effect on career dynamics. For example, technology took away the need for 13 column spreadsheets and manual bookkeeping. This shift impacted those in the accounting industry in the mid-eighties and early nineties.

Online banking and photo snapshots of deposits are taking away the dependency of manpower needs within financial institutions. These are just two industries but there are many others.

As technology advances, we must reinvent our career packaging because the needs for the three career paradigms are impacted. Typically, the impact starts, at the transactional level and then moving upward. Change is so rapid that we must be fully aware of who we are. Since we are all products of our past, our awareness of where we are from and how we reached our current pinnacle impacts the way we react to the forces of change. No matter the level we have to be equipped with tools to respond to change within the environment or we lose out on the opportunities which exist at that moment.

The universe responds to the demands we put on the self. Knowledge of who we are impacts our ability to be free. Bondage occurs when we rely on others to tell us who we are, what we know, and what our next moves can be. Since we were all put on the earth for a purpose, it is in finding that purpose that we find the guidance to the discovery of what we should do. Discovery depends on situations and outcomes you desire. It starts with where and what you spend the majority of your free time doing.

For years researchers have tried to help man in finding himself. The results of that have been batteries of self-assessments that help us to examine who we are. Don't complete them as you think others would want to see you but as you see yourself. We have to see our self retrospectively as well as prospectively, meaning our past and possible self.

The goal of the book is to increase career management education awareness and understanding of what it takes to have a sustainable career, achieve the economic dream and survival in the 21st century age of technology and globalization. Educating the audience on the personal behaviors and actions needed to achieve the paradigm shift from general skills in office, processing and manufacturing skills to one with a combination of specific and craftsman like talents, able to effectively communicate, able to adapt and blend in the areas of technology, math, science and engineering combined with different general skills in such areas of communication, flexibility, innovative, problem resolution and critical thinking.

Processing and manufacturing driven work models were great and helped to build our middle class. However, the paradigm has shifted to one where creative, innovative and critical thinkers with solution oriented models must exist in order to remain competitive in 21st technology driven work settings. The pendulum shifts from worker mindset to entrepreneurial mindsets, with enhancements in knowledge to match that of technology. A new type of worker not afraid of change and the willingness to change as needed to keep pace with desired path of passion and profession. In order to achieve the goals of the text, it is divided into ten chapters.

Chapter one is the introduction to the components of Professional Freedom. Chapter 2, "Why Professional Freedom," serves as a framework for reinvention and professional freedom provides an overview of the importance of reinvention. Chapter 3, "The Twelve Components Defined," breaks down the 12 components and defines key terms. In addition it provides the knowledge background of the current global work environment, changes in technology and its impact on the workforce. The text provides the components of professional freedom and the benefits of each component and ends with examples of an individual who exemplifies professional freedom.

Chapter 4, "Research Findings and Rationale," takes a deep dive into the core components of Professional Freedom. It provides the reader with reasons why each component is necessary and important. The section ends with examples of professionally free individuals around the world. Chapter 5, "The Art of Reinventing," provides the reader with insists into quest for ongoing change of self in order to remain a sustainable force in the work market space. Chapter 6, provides a reinvention checklist to test the audience readiness for reinvention.

Chapter 7 "Preparing for the change," takes the reader through the awareness of upcoming change and the preliminary processes and thinking patterns needed to prepare for the upcoming change. Chapter 8 "Mastering the Layoff," or "The Right Way to Get Fired," is my story of living through the challenges faced by many in the 21st century world of work. This section shares how being prepared with an exit strategy helps to smooth the transition to new opportunities as well as reduces the stresses associated with layoffs, downsizings, and restructures. Many of the processes are at the core of Professional Freedom. Through implementation helped to provide a base for living the style of life and working within my passion.

The reader will journey 31 days through my layoff experience with me. Each day I share personal as well as prescriptive actions though stories of day to day actions. I share Professional Freedom Tips, (**PFTIPS**) to use, worksheets and exercises for the reader to help begin the process of becoming Professionally Free. Chapter 9, "Professional Freedom Transition Checklist," provides the reader with a tool to test their level of Professional Freedom.

The final chapter, 10 "Bringing it All Together," ties the uniqueness of the twelve components of Professional Freedom in helping the author to live a life of passion, life works, meaning and experiencing a career in a more meaningful and focused manner. This leads to the true measure of success in an ever changing world of work. The text also serves as an guide in helping the reading audience to see that it is the way in which you accept and embrace change that will determine your outcome.

WHY PROFESSIONAL FREEDOM

Today's workers are finding the pressures brought on by changes in the workforce and the uncertainty of not knowing if there will be employment opportunities day to day stressful and difficult to master. Some are finding that they are more adaptive to others. While others can't seem to make heads of tails of which career avenues are sustainable and worth seeking. Managing career shift changes means understanding the various dynamics of career education and preparation.

Pressures sounding career change include technology, smart phone applications, available use of knowledge, globalization of markets, changes in the nature of the workforce, and the new paradigm of knowledge, innovation and creativity needed throughout the workforce to handle the rapid changes organizations are experiencing. Education is necessary but it is only a small part of your career equation. There are many other facets which determine what role you can ultimately play in this game we call life.

The economic theory of workers as resource is now workers as an investment in capital. Having the right capital to fulfill immediate and long term needs requires a worker who is ready to contribute on entry. One who is already trained in the core skills, knowledge and abilities with the right amount of soft skills and personal social capital for short term as well as long term results.

Building on "Who I know," "What I know," and "Who I am" as foundational components to achieving career longevity and success in a time of rapid change. While helping the audience build a sustainable career action plan that is unique for the individual.

We are creatures of habit. Our habits influence our ability to change or not. As humans we have a desire to advance in life. However, some times our habits prohibit our advancement. Therefore advancement is dependent upon how deliberate we are in our efforts to advance and what we categorize as advancement. Our efforts therefore establish our ability to change, progress, and move in the direction of our purpose.

Professional Freedom is based on our ability to discover, develop goals, implement goals, and become fluid in our ability to make changes needed. We have the ability to actively mold our career future. At any point in time we will be dealt a hand that must be played. We must remember even the worst hand at the table can win. The art of how we play based on the possibilities is shaped by levels of Professional Freedom even in the Midst of Chaos.

Professional Freedom in the Midst of Chaos is a distinctive guide to building a sustainable career path. It takes the best practice methodology based on research and experience. It is intended for use as a text and course in career management education and development, and personal growth. The distinctiveness of Professional Freedom lies in the combination of real life experiences, research and practice methodology linking components of new world of employment, economic theory, psychology, business, life skills, special learning features and an active engaging material demonstration.

The text is a 21st century approach to career and personal development with a primary emphasis on individual growth and professional freedom. Based on a formula of knowledge+skills+abilities+passion=potential+preference+power+positioning=interest. In order to build the formula the text integrates concepts and practices of four capital components— intellectual, social, political, and psychological. The text then combines the capital components with individual talents, personal branding, values, social responsibility, and financial stability.

THE 12 COMPONENTS DEFINED

Keys to Career Freedom

Every discovery gives life meaning. It is a process of knowing who we are, where we are, who we know, what we know and the value of our network and time. Reinvention is a process of being aware of transitions and transformations. It is a process of necessary growth that starts from the beginning of life, work, and career to middle age and beyond. A process of adding to what we know in order to build and create a unique path of opportunity specially geared to the individual.

The most basic principle of life is change. People, work, business, industry, and the world are forever changing. It is the act of growth and improvement. Without change the end comes sooner rather than later. The new economy is constantly changing. With this change comes new ways of doing things, reducing the amount of manpower needed in what used to be a process driven society. The ability to be flexible and nimble in, knowledge, action and commitment, is a must. The ability to be proactive in changing based on the constant demands of new economy. This is reinvention. Every change gives life and career new meaning.

The capacity to be flexible and nimble in knowledge and commitment are the new rules of the day. A reinvention expert (needed for economic survival) is a teachable change agent who is capable of learning from mistakes with a willingness to invest time and the necessary resources in professional development. This person lives a life of passion, potential, preference and has the right positioning power, while earning the necessary income needed to pursue goals in life. Professional Freedom, means having a different spectrum, a career life filled with experiences of autonomy independence, free will, self-determination, and self-sufficiency. Professionally Free individuals are qualified, proficient, and skilled. They are resilient, optimistic, and self-aware. They are fully engaged, motivated, creative, innovative and more productive workforce members. There are twelve foundational components that make up Professional Freedom, (PF). They are as follows:

Intellectual Capital (IC) = Education and knowledge of core areas of interest combined with talent and abilities

Social Capital (SC) = Strong base of individuals, groups, organizations and teams to link and connect them to the proper resources based on need as well as being a strong resource for others within core network. Good use of social media as mechanism to enhance brand awareness.

Political Capital (POC) = Strength in making connections internally, externally, across geographies, through affiliations to capture audiences needed for success.

Psychological Capital, (PsyCap) = Positive levels of hope, optimism, self-efficacy and resilience as the emotional and behavioral component needed to provide a strong foundation for the other components of Professional Freedom.

Relevant Talent (RT) = Core skills, abilities and experience in the primary areas of chosen profession. Can easy adapt, change and blend skills to adjust to career market conditions.

Change Competency- (CC) = understanding the necessary components needed to effectively make changes no matter the situation. Identifying the signs and signals of when a career change is needed.

Brand Awareness (BA) =your audience can easily identify with who you are and the core skills sets, behaviors, values, and personal image you personify.

Social Responsibility (SR)=Effectively utilizing other seven core competencies to enhance the community where you live and work in order to build a stronger and more resilient community for living of all at various economic levels.

Financial Stability (FS) =How to manage income effectively. Using financial resources to live successfully. How to take what you have to make the most out it. Can adequately meet the daily basic financial needs required to provide food, shelter and clothing. Not living on bonuses, overtime pay or second income. Not spending more than 60% of pay on living expenses.

Self-Assessments =Knowledge of self and personal preferences such tests as AMA DISC, VARK Learning Styles, Career Test, Career Values Test, Personality Test, and Jung Personality Test

Time Management = Understanding how to effectively use time. This includes knowledge of how you currently spend your time. How to calculate time spent and missed opportunities due to ineffective use of time.

Goal Setting – How to set SMART goals, establish and build goals that are obtainable, measurable and results oriented

Every discovery I have made through PF helps me to understand my relationship to myself and the world in which I work. It provides me with the ability to secure capital needed for current and future lifestyle and personal goals. Beginning with self-knowledge, I became aware of my passions and what I was willing to do each day for personal freedom. What came naturally to me but seemed complex to others, the ability to grow through observations of challenges and comments of others, helped me to discover challenges that became opportunities. The things and situations that drove me became the fuel for my change engine. Staying the course to pursue my dreams and ambitions took discovery, self-knowledge, disclosure, failure, time, acceptance and observations.

We all have growth needs, but are we aware of all of them or not? This is the question we must ask? The culture we live in determines and influences our ability to become PF. Therefore reinvention becomes paramount to successful integration into the new culture driven by technology, globalization and rapid change. Today's culture impacts the ways we work and seek employment opportunities in a world primarily dominated by capitalism and free enterprise.

Due to continued advances in technology that characterize the next phase of workforce requirements, training is needed. However training is expensive, and who best fits the needed training is an anomaly for many employers. Companies are in business to produce profits as such they look to find the best talent to help achieve their profit goals. They are not experienced at developing talent to produce said profits. Due to the rapid changes in technology advancements, employers are not fully aware of the talent needs thus, they are unwilling to spend the necessary capital to upgrade internal talent for asset they are not sure will return a profit. Therefore, many feel that it is better to bring in talent as needed and lay off talent lacking in skills, knowledge and abilities no longer needed.

In addition the paradigm has shifted in manpower needs. What use to take 30 people to do now may only require six? What use to take a year to achieve takes only weeks? Yes, technology is great but it comes with a cost. One we have not fully figured out how to master other than to start with the known, the individual.

Since we live in a world dominated and connected by technology, we have to develop the knowledge, skills and abilities to operate and compete successfully at our own expense. Yes, that is correct we cannot depend on employers to provide the tools we need to be competitive in the market place. Why? Because we are free to sell our services in a talent competitive market place based on supply and demand.

It's the basic concept of supply and demand. Employers must replenish their workforce with the right relevant talent and skills needed to compete with the global market. With every new product or service, the larger the need for the need for talent to administer, regulate and maintain the growth and development of said product or service. Therefore, understanding the market needs is important to the individual career seeker. You can readily reshape yourself to the constantly changing demands of the market place;

You have "changeable behavior," –Hopeful, enthusiastic, resilient, and optimist.

You have a vision and mission that is flexible to the ever changing market demands.

You have mastered several possibilities for your career direction.

RESEARCH FINDINGS AND RATIONALE

Blending of Research Findings

We live in a time of hyper-competitive markets, numerous changes are taking place that are changing the playing field for individuals both seeking to obtain and/or maintain employment. There is a need to always be ready to move in order to stay employed. This is a change in the way you manage your career. The increasing fluidity in work opportunities requires that career seekers build and protect their talent offerings in order to remain competitive in the market.

The changing employment environment has also provided a large audience of downsized and reduction in force talent pools unaware of how to build sustainability measures during these periods of high unemployment. This has impacted the ability to maintain live styles and future income opportunities.

Professional Freedom is based on the economic principles of capital accu2mulation; investment, talent deployment, and value creation associated with intellectual, political, social and psychological capital. Knowledge of how to leverage, your capital is crucial to career management. Your implicit knowledge adds to your unique talent value proposition. You own this knowledge and are responsible for updating it continually for maximum success. Professionally Free individuals are self-directed towards the goal of achieving personal success based on the 12 core foundational principals of; Intellectual Capital (IC), Social Capital (SC), Political Capital (POC), Psychological Capital, (PsyCap), Relevant Talent (RT), Change Competency- (CC), Brand Awareness (BA), Social Responsibility (SR, Financial Stability (FS), Self-Assessments, Time Management, and Goal Setting.

Intellectual Capital (IC)

Education and knowledge of core areas of interest must be combined with the talent and abilities in order to perform successfully in any industry of choice. Intellectual capital is a necessity. It provides the competitive advantage for career seeking individuals. Intellectual capital includes knowledge, skills, and abilities often referred to as *KSAs*. Intellectual capital also includes education level, industry experience and project management or management related experience.

Research completed by Lodestar for Operation ABLE of Michigan in combination with the Kellogg Foundation on career resiliency through their creation of assessment tools as well as the Organization for Training and Development have shown a direct relationship between intellectual capital and an individual's survival and/or growth in the employment market. It is directly related to your competitive advantage. How you communicate and show your knowledge in your branding and marketing tools (resume, business cards and dress).

Individuals with higher levels of intellectual capital experience higher earnings and income levels than those with lower or untrained abilities to communicate effectively. In order to remain competitive, continuous improvement in capital including developing new KSAs is imperative.

Time in time again individuals with the right KSAs have a direct link to continued success periods of economic shifts. Examples of those with strong intellectual capital include; Steve Jobs, Dianne Sawyer, Oprah Winfrey, or Bill Gates. Time after time none of the four were happy with the status quo, they sought additional KSA's in the way of product enhancements and improvements of self and those around them to capitalize on growth opportunities. Each understood that the knowledge they started with would not be enough to continue to grow in order to reach their goals.

Social Capital (SC)

Social Capital is a network quality social contacts who have access and political positioning to open doors and or provide valuable information on career and business related opportunities. Social Capital has a direct impact of the receipt of job information. Individuals with an extensive social network capable of providing access to prestigious job positions or business opportunities have shown to be the most successful in their career pursuits. Social Capital has shown to be the determinant in those who make it and those who don't. The right social capital facilitates the receipt of job leads, as does the daily interactions within the right networks whether physical or cyber ally connected.

Research studies completed McDonald, Lin and AO, showed a direct correlation between social capital, career success and job seeking candidates success of job candidates who landed positions verses others and found that due their strong social networks those with the right social capital were more successful at seeking and landing career positions and opportunities than those without social capital.

Studies have also shown a direct correlation between pay and income. Strong social capital equipped individuals with the ability to build and seek the right opportunities. Ties to the right people lead to growth faster than having the relevant talent, skills, or education. Professionally Free individuals have a strong base of individuals, groups, organizations and teams to link to. They understand that who you know directly impacts your value proposition in and out of organizations.

The value of relationships between people and networks are developed over time and must be continuously nurtured. Relationships we form with others impact our ability to make career moves. In addition our ability to connect others as an influence impacts our value as seen by possible future employers or starting a new business or venture. This means maintaining strong ties to others and having connections is important to career success.

Those with high social capital form relationships with others in similar professions, within the community, and of shared personal values linked organizations. This impacts their transitional opportunities and transactional value. They know how to connect them with the proper resources based on their individual needs. They are also a strong resource for others within their core network.

Good use of social media is a mechanism to enhance brand awareness. Social networks are an important aspect of career management. The advent technology provides many ways to stay connected, although the more people you have in your network does not necessarily mean that you achieve results faster.

Electronic social networking is continuing to grow. There is still growth and knowledge in the impact and effects of social media on career dynamics. However, if we fail to use this asset properly it could cause unwanted circumstances on careers. Some of the popular social media sites for careers are LinkedIn and Facebook. Both have existed for less than 10 years. A healthy social networking portfolio should consist of each of the following:

- Family (immediate and extended) providing emotional support, and friendship
- Personal friendships- those closest to and know you the best, providing emotional and constructive feedback
- Past and previous employers-managers, leaders, HR, etc.
- Trade or professional groups
- Your professional peer group
- Professionals in your local and regional areas
- Religious or social community groups
- College Professors, High School Teachers, Coaches or Counselors
- Team Members you have previously work with on major projects
- School Alumni members
- Virtual Relationships- online projects peers, those connected with online with a history of interactions

Remember you need people on the field for coaching, guiding, and providing valuable input on your game. They must understand you and what you bring to the table and can easily vouch for you. They are your sponsors, coaches and or mentors providing you with challenging assignments and exposure to opportunities which would otherwise be limited. Be careful of the fair weather spectators in stands, those who cheer you on only when winning but lose faith in your efforts when you are losing. Remember you want fans not spectators. Examples of those with high levels of social capital include: Michael Strahan, Barbara Walters, John Elway, Oprah Winfrey, and Bill Clinton to name a few as well as those leading well known professional and social organizations.

Political Capital (POC)

Political Capital is defined as the ability to effectively understand others in working relationships and use that knowledge to influence others to act in ways that enhance your personal goals and objectives. Studies around career success and earnings power have shown a strong relationship to political capital. Individuals who are savvy in political capital have strength in making the right connections internally, externally, and across geographies, through affiliations to capture audiences needed for success.

Studies completed by Todd, Harris, Harris and Wheeler all determined the outcomes of political capital on career success. The outcomes of total compensations, promotions, career satisfaction, life satisfaction and job mobility combined with networking ability all had a direct relationship to career outcomes. The key characteristics of these influencers are confidence and optimism, relevant skills, experiences, behavior, integrity, ethics, their ability to influence others they have no power over. The charisma possessed by such individuals leads to favorable work conditions, and their personal well-being.

Professional Free individuals are politically savvy and understand how to remove roadblocks that impede growth. They understand the power of connections and search for influencers to help them move bigger blocks. In increasing rewards, they may give occasional encouragement or pave the way with gold.

Individuals with political capital have the following practices;

- They make quality contacts with people within the organization
- They are honest
- They listen to advice and accept constructive feedback
- They enjoy people
- They practice effective listening skills
- They speak only when they have something to contribute
- They like finding the good in others and complimenting them accordingly

In addition, they are self-aware of how their personal communication style influences others. They have a diverse network of people who can use their emotional intelligence, social knowledge and persuasion, social competence and skills to influence others to effectively gain entrance into new markets and career territories. Examples of individuals with political capital include previous and current presidents, executive leadership in organizations, popular television shows.

Psychological Capital, (PsyCap)

Research completed by Luthans, Youssef, Avolio, Mastern, Rousseau, Bandra, Seligman and others have shown that the components of an individual's Psychological Capital has a direct relationship in situations where success outcomes are greater when faced with adversity and uncertainty. The turn of the 21st century has many in the job market unsure and uneasy about their career prospects and longevity in current and future career matters.

Positive levels of hope, optimism, self-efficacy and resilience as the emotional and behavioral component needed to provide a strong foundation for the other components of Professional Freedom.

Psychological capital "an individual's positive psychological state of development and is characterized by:

(1) Having confidence (self- efficacy) to take on and put in the necessary effort to succeed at challenging tasks;

(2) Making a positive attribution (optimism) about succeeding now and in the future;

(3) Persevering towards goals and, when necessary, redirecting paths to goals (hope) in order to succeed; and

(4) When beset by problems and adversity, sustaining and bouncing back even beyond (resilience) to attain success".

The positive psychological capacities of confidence, optimism, hope, and resilience are key attributes in individuals who have achieved career success. Research findings in career management show that positive emotions and thoughts among successful athletes and leaders inspired continued growth and knowledge of attributes towards successful career transitions.

Self-aware individuals understand purpose, passion and self-motivators direct their behaviors. My research findings conclude that an individual's true self must be evaluated in terms of values and ethics when used to influence motivations. In order to have resilient organization we must have resilient employees.

Resilient employees view challenges as opportunities to grow, learn and achieve new results. A focus on positive individual features, experiences, personal traits, and the workplace enhance productivity as well as personal and organizational well-being.

Research suggests that workplace resilience prompts self-efficacy, control, persistence and reduces anxiety. Other researchers in career management and training have identified that the true self provided individuals with a mechanism to specify personal values that allow them the ability to speak their true voice. Along with discussions on self-motivation as personal strivings, benchmarks for success, and idealized visions-- all of which have an impact on self-views of the possible self. Self-view and possible self as reflections are important to an individual's identification. This same concept affects the individual view of the possible self. The self-view as described by each of the theorists helps to build upon the principles and core competencies seen in the individuals with professional freedom. Examples of individuals who display a positive psychological capital include: The William Sisters (Venus and Serena), Bill and Hillary Clinton, John Elway, Nelson Mandela, and Ellen Degeneres.

Relevant Talent (RT)

Relevant Talent is the core skills, abilities and experience in the primary area of chosen profession. These individuals can easy adapt, change and blend skills to adjust to career market conditions. They do this by engaging in continuous learning opportunities through seminars, professional associations, reading, volunteering and stepping up for challenging projects. Research suggests that relevant factors that make individuals valuable in their current context include:

- Specialized knowledge, skills, and experience
- Personal skills and behaviors, potential to grow and contributions at high levels,
- Personal productivity in relation to stakeholder value, and alignment with organizational values.
- Technical/Professional competencies include coaching, leading, communication skills, decision making, planning and organizing, teamwork and collaboration.
- Administrative and Office includes adaptability, building positive working relationships, continuous improvement, contributing to team success and managing work.

Effective career management has become a crucial component of an individual's career survival. Talent relevancy allows you the ability to negotiate job transfers, obtain development opportunities more easily, build networks and develop intangible assets. Examples of individuals who display this competency include; Marissa Mayer, Alicia Keys, Virginia Rometty, and Denzel Washington. These individuals have successfully moved from transactional to technical or tactical levels in their careers. However famous or levels of CEO they have earned the same concepts applies to individuals in the day to day grind from entry level positions to mid-to senior level positions. These individuals are called on often to help with projects and increasing levels of responsibility and accountability.

Change Competency (CC)

Change is a given. The "universe is change," Marcus Aurelius Antonius, (120-180 A.D.) believed that our life is what our thoughts make it. Change is no surprise or new phenomenon in and of itself but it is the rapidness of change that shifts the paradigm from gradual, with time for preparation, to rapid continuous change. In this type of change those impacted must be prepared.

Due to the advancements in technology and globalization practices, rapid change have impacted the way we work, positions needed, and organizational structures. This has left our workforce unprepared. A change which calls for immediate action in order for the worker to understand and manage his/her career for sustainability in the current economic environment.

Individuals must understand the necessary components needed to effectively make changes no matter the situation and be able to identify the signs and signals of when a career change is needed. The theory of evolution provides the premise that we are all products of our past. As we evolve, so must our ability to take control of our careers. Your needs will differ at various stages of your career. Before you reach the job loss stage you have to be willing to change your way of thinking and start visualizing yourself accomplishing something different, something grander. Remember people don't just get what they want by being lucky. It's about being prepared when an opportunity presents itself. A loss of a job is one of those opportunities.

The current job market conditions built with layoffs, downsizing, outsourcing, and company failures have career seeking individuals wondering "what does it take" to get a job, get paid for what they are worth, have employment security and like where they work to the point of satisfaction and engagement.

Having a successful and sustainable career means being versatile as your needs change and the economic employment market changes. You must have the tools needed even in the midst of a twenty-first century chaotic career state of affairs.

Remaining in the employability game takes continuous reinvention. Being highly engaged in career pursuits eliminates or minimizes career frustrations, burnout and disappointment. Sustainable careers now require an emphasis on continuous learning, skill enhancement and career development which leads to building skills that help balance or advance your career. This leads to increase pay, reward opportunities, and maximized earning potential.

Freedom of choice to accept current conditions or make a change can only occur when you are prepared to compete competitively. Having the necessary talent with the necessary tools or systems to help in setting career goals, and laying out plans for achieving those goals helps one master continuous change and improvement in knowledge.

Knowledge and aligning your talent portfolio for maximum success while coordinating the right social and political resources when needed. Continuous development and accumulation of additional knowledge and skills are needed for future career growth.

This book has hopefully demonstrated the need for an effective career management program; how to increase your effectiveness in the job market; how knowledge of key strengths; management of time, financial strength, and goal setting are all components of your talent offering. Examples of this include; top athletes, top entertainers, Nobel Prize winners, and experts within their individual careers.

Brand Awareness (BA)

Brand awareness means your audience can easily identify with who you are and the core skills sets, behaviors, values, and personal image you personify. Personal branding is a personal marketing and advertisement process used to establish with your audience who you are (personal) and what you do (career) and how successful you are at what you do. Personal branding combines your digital, work, and public presentations to the world.

The image you present tells your audience who you are and where you are. Your image encompasses everything you do—what you wear, how you sound, your patterns of behavior, how others see you, how they identify you, those you follow and associate yourself with.

Branding models can also include items such as the way you dress, hair style, weight, size, extracurricular activities and education. Again, it relates to how others see you. Communication factors and personal hygiene are other factors crucial to branding. Examples of those with strong brand awareness includes; Kim Kardashian, Steve Harvey, CNN, Fox and ABC News Franchises, McDonald's Nike, Michael Jordon, and Lebron James to name just a few. Brand recognition is important due to the associations, character, and recognitions it builds for the brand holder. It takes a lot to build a brand but it only takes seconds or one or two wrong moves to ruin your brand. Brand is also linked heavily with financial capital and the ability to build additional capital.

Social Responsibility (SR)

We all share in the responsibility in helping to build and sustain the environments we earn and live within. Social responsibility is means utilizing one's talents, skills, abilities, and available resources to advance the causes, needs and better the good of the communities where you live and work. As businesses within our communities change in size, demographics and structure the needs of the community become more prevalent and impactful on individual talents, resources and time. This has created gaps and voids left by organizations and government which need to be filled resources from the community.

Effectively utilizing the other seven core competencies to enhance the community where you live and work in order to build a stronger and more resilient community. Many of the gaps can be filled by the community of talent coming together to help resolve the immediate and most pressing needs by giving of their time, talent and resources.

The result benefits of the giving community includes building a more sustainable community, increase in community awareness, talent enhancements, increasing social network, political capital through leadership, enhancing branding and helping in building a more resilient, hopeful and optimistic community. Another benefit which has been experienced by many givers is more of a focus on areas of impact in the community they are more passionate about, like homelessness, education, income disparity, financial responsibility, and literacy all which impact direction of the current and future trends in the community.

We must consciously make an effort to provide our fair share of time, talent and resources to help those who have not reached the levels of self-sufficiency needed to be contributing members of the community. We all share in the role of community obligations, philanthropy, and paternalism. Therefore, we must work together to alleviate community problems, civic improvements, and contribute to the economic interest of community programs which impact the sustainability of our community.

The benefits gained from giving of time, talent and resources outweigh the investment of three due to the 360 degree impact it has on the community economic stability. For example; a community of givers can change the how resources for community of those less fortunate in receiving education, and living resources has been shown to cut down on crime in the community.

Crime is a costly expense for any community the more a community can impact the effects of crime the more time and resources the community can use on challenges brought on by natural disasters and infrastructure needs. Or another example, in education includes the types of jobs and careers are available in a community based on the educational achievements of the talent resources.

We see the impact from givers such as the Bill Gates Foundation, the United Way, Boys and Girls Clubs and Girls and Boy Scouts, Court Appointed Special Advocates, American Cancer Society and more. Without individual givers of time, talent or treasure these organizations would not benefit the communities at the levels capable of achieving sustainable outcomes. So time and resources matter to you and your community because it enhances both you and your community.

Financial Stability (FS)

According to research on the biggest personal stresses to success and personal growth opportunities is financial. In order to stay in the game you have to manage what you have and make the most of it at that given point and time. You must manage income effectively and use financial resources to live successfully. Financial stability for the purpose of this text means having the right amount cash flow needed to get the necessary resources to keep you professionally free from decisions which impact your health, (stress) and well-being. This means having the capital or resources needed to educate, gain skills, and additional abilities to move self in direction of your goals.

Based on discussions with students and colleagues over the years their finances was number one in keeping them from achieving their dreams and callings in life. Many stated that they were in careers because they needed a paycheck and benefits and not because it was something they wanted to do.

Do you understand how to take what you have to make the most out it? Can you adequately meet the daily basic financial needs required to provide food, shelter and clothing without living on bonuses, overtime pay or second income or spending more than 60% of pay on living expenses?

The new economic environment is built with layoffs, downsizing and organizational restructures. The booming eighties and nineties have left many in state of income shock. Gone are the days for many of stock options and nice bonuses which made many live beyond their imaginary dreams. Gone are the two homes, nice vacations, cars and cash beyond imagination. This is 2012 and for many incomes of yesterday are gone along with the investments of yesterday day. Many have lost either one or both homes because of failure to capture and live within goals and preparation for the future. We lived in the now. Those who thought that they prepared based their investments on unsound practices.

As we made more we spent more. We upsized our homes, and our lives but we failed to upsize our investment in self while income was flowing. We spent an enormous amount money on children and keeping them what we thought was happy while we earned and spent more. We must now learn from the mistakes of our past and start include our living desires within our goals for the future. Always keeping the following formula at the forefront. Savings, Investments, Values and Goals =Yields Sustainability.

Our economic environment will continue to change for the foreseeable future. We must always be prepared and ready for downsizing, restructures, and layoffs. Which means having the right amount needed in savings for 6-12 months or more of no income. The right combination of sound investments for future income needs. A strong base of values to live by so that those values presented by outside pressures like the media and those with more. Measuring success by your unique set of values. Understanding and equipped with the knowledge on how each decision you make impacts your financial footprint. Finally, having goals which keep in mind where you are going and when you plan to get there and what you will do once those goals are achieved.

Self-Assessments

Self-assessments help to stimulate your interest by helping you to go deeper into the aspects of you. Where you stand in relationship to the areas the assessments test for provides a guide for ways to improve as well awareness of areas which may hinder communications, relationships, teamwork, learning, values, leadership styles, work styles and career acumen.

Self-assessments combined with the other components of Professional Freedom helps you to find out what type of career, workplace values and quality of work conditions that fit your lifestyle. Assessments are important components to development because they help to identify areas of external or work related motivators and intrinsic or self-related motivators. As management experts and researcher training literature suggests, the behaviors associated with successful career management serve as a mechanism for unlocking human potential. Knowledge of those behaviors is therefore important making career assessment tools vital to discovery of who we are.

Career management practices combine your motivations, needs and wants into competencies, interpersonal skills, emotional intelligence, values, and sense of self. Therefore, the need to use instruments that tests for behaviors and how they impact career decisions is useful for effective career management observation and training programs.

Time Management

Research shows that individuals with bad time management skills are less likely to achieve success even when having all the other necessary skills and attributes to be successful. Time management is a soft skill that many individuals lack. They can't see the forest for the trees because trees keep getting in their way. Good time management skills starts with understanding your macro and micro goals. Without goals we fly in many directions because we have no plans to what we want our career future to look like. Many students stop attending college due to time management challenges.

Career achievement is dependent upon many factors we have discussed to this point however those factors cannot be achieved without an adequate awareness and knowledge of the benefits of effective time management practices. Effective time management involves an adequate allocation of time, resource management, and knowledge of earnings potential and the elimination of procrastination.

Freedom of opportunity cannot happen if there is no time to prepare for that freedom. Technology has come on the scene to enhance our life by providing less time due to the amount of resources it takes now compared previously to complete a task. For example, it takes me five minutes to pay monthly bills now compared to 30-45 minutes previously. Another example, I can now work from home instead of driving to the office saving me a three hour roundtrip commute a day based on traffic or a total annual savings of 720 hours. Between paying bills and computing to work I have saved 740 hours which I chose to use on increasing my education. That improvement increased with options in talent markets which lead to other opportunities. In addition to education I gain more time 240 hours of the 740 to spend on family, friends, community and self.

How you currently spend your time and the cost of that time spent? What opportunity costs are you foregoing due to time spent doing something else? Understanding where and how you spend your time is just as critical as understanding how you spend your available financial resources because both impact the other.

Allocating your time properly to gain and sustain career success means managing your most valuable resource, time. As stated earlier technology can be your best competitive advantage for gaining access to opportunities. An example of how I achieve success in managing my time effectively is through carefully evaluating on monthly bases how I spent my time the previous month. In my review are seven core areas: Income producing items, non-income producing items, items someone could have done and time spent verses potential income lost, family time, personal time, rest and relaxation, time spent investing in capital (intellectual, social, political, and financial).

A rule of thumb I live by is not touching any item or task more than once. Also, master the art of non-procrastination. Procrastination impacts time management due to the actions it takes not completing a task, regretting that you must perform the task and putting other tasks before the task you are procrastinating over. Time management is a soft skill that must be mastered in order to achieve the success you deserve and seek. Master your time and be rewarded, however if your time masters you be prepared for chaos and uncertainty in your life and career.

Goal Setting

Goal Setting is establishing realistic expectations and timelines for achieving something which is important to you. The importance can be based on several factors but one of the most import is you and how it takes you or gets you closer to something you want to achieve. There is nothing you cannot achieve if you want it enough. Goal setting is an important aspect of Professional Freedom.

There are five principal components to goal setting. The goal must be specific, measurable, attainable, realistic, and time bound. In order to create something new and different there must be a goal. Goals allow you to do something you have never done before by preparing you to make it happen. Setting SMART goals provides a mechanism for achieving said goals. First start by establishing and building goals that are obtainable, measurable and results oriented? The first step is be specific about what is you want to accomplish. What will the results look like? Can your goal be achieved, meaning has this been done before? Do you have or can you obtain the necessary resources to act on this goal? In what time frame can the goal be achieved?

Another important factor about goal setting is being aware of the type of goal you want. For example, an educational goal is long term because it typically takes more than 6 months to achieve. Whereas a goal around buying educational material which cost less than $25.00 can be seen as a short term goal, provided that $25.00 is amount that is easily obtainable and available for making the purchase.

When setting career goals it always important to be realistic. Research the career using such sites as Onet.gov or DOL job skills and potential career future sites. Complete your own investigations and not that of schools or others who don't have your personal career interest. Remember this, You and only you can master what is best for you, other are there to provide input but in order to be successful it must begin with you.

Start with what you know, what skills and abilities you have. What skills are required, what are the possible companies in need of and hiring is in demand? Who do you know in your social network? Can they lead you to someone with hiring authority? Can this someone give value to your potential in the company? What potential does the position promise? What is the growth trajectory of the career field?

THE ART OF REINVENTING

Pain Points Signs for Change

My Journey through life has been a series of reinventions, each one beginning with milestones, based on chaos, hard lessons, and the realities of life. However, I chose to focus on the positives of each situation which serve to guide me to improvements. Each milestone I make represents pain points, leading me to where I need to be. These pain points enlighten me to opportunities for self-improvements which point to a need for change. The changes I make are based on new knowledge acquired through education, experience and envisioning what can be. What can bear various possibilities; some stronger and with more potential than others. Each possibility of strength is pivotal to my next reinvention and each reinvention bringing me one step closer to what and where I am destined to be. I start by sharing the following real life stories.

It's the middle of an August night and I have to be up soon for my flight back to Atlanta, Georgia from Richmond, Virginia.

I am in Richmond to train for a campus dean position. While here, I serve as a full-time Professor on campus in order to gain a better perspective of how a campus works. I lecture a Thursday night Capstone Course on Business Strategies for MBA students in their final course of study before graduation. Earlier this evening, at the end of class, two students asked to see me to discuss their frustration with finding the right employment opportunity that fit their educational backgrounds. They are hoping that getting an MBA would help in opening new doors of opportunity.

They are both currently employed. However they are unhappy with their current positions and want to make sure that they move in the right direction after graduation. Both have undergraduate degrees from a local well known university. One is a political science graduate and working as a grocery store manager for a low end grocery chain. The other is a computer engineering graduate working as computer analyst for a voter tabulation software company. This is our eighth week of classes together and over this time I have noticed some things which may be hindering their career growth.

I understand what the students are going through. There have been many other stories, shared with me by students, friends, family, and associates, of the inability to move forward in their careers. The pain they suffer by having to work a particular job because they need to survive, the overwhelming stress in their life due to working for and reporting to managers who can't help them because the managers don't understand how to help. Not having a clear career path before leaving college, not understanding how to brand themselves, how to take their knowledge, skills, and experience to turn it into opportunities which blend with their specific values. Not understanding that each phase in life brings with it change and that the type of change needed is based on the current environment they must adapt to survive in. We all have a purpose in life, finding it and capturing the opportunities that our innate talents offer us start with changing and expanding the positive attributes which complement our talents. We must reinvent.

It takes reinvention to build career sustainability. I am not saying start over, but you have do more than just a tune-up, which is simply getting back to where you started and liked what you were doing. It is important to understand if what you have been doing has not helped you achieve the success you desire, reinvention is necessary. Envision where you want to be; see what is lacking; build upon the positive; and capitalize on your unique natural talents to lead to where you are destined to be.

I have since childhood unknowingly had the capacity to bounce back from adversity. As a child of a fourteen year old mother, living in poverty there were many opportunities to fail but each time I have chosen the path less chosen by those in similar situations. When faced with adversity having the right tools in place is paramount to a successful transition from the known to unknown. This leads me to the passion and belief I have in the power of reinvention. Reinvention is your path to Professional Freedom.

REINVENTION CHECKLIST

Discover, Build, Adapt, and Fluid

Reinvention involves four pillars — Discovery, Building, Adaptability, and Pliability

Discovery- Exploring yourself

Who Am I? What would I do for free?

What makes me unique?

What are my talents?

What skills and training do I have?

What type of network do I have? Who do I know? How can they help? Are they willing to help?

What do others think about me? What type of influence do I have? In what settings?

If conditions were different, I see myself as being this, what is this?

Build – Engaging in the art of you

Start by assembling the possibilities for you. Clearly define what you want.

Mold and form the top three potentials.

What is your personal brand, (how do you want the world to see you and know you)?

Is what you want obtainable? If not now, is it in the future? If so, how long before reaching it.

What compromises are you willing to make?

What do you value, i.e. Type of employment, location, benefits, growth, job flexibility? What is important to you, i.e. family, religion, hours of work, work schedule?

Develop an action plan for reaching the possibilities.

In order to reach my desired state what do I need, i.e. additional knowledge, skills, networking, resources, and education?

Adaptability- Being able to adjust readily to different conditions now that you know who you are and the possible opportunities

Can you change and adapt to new and different circumstances and situations?

Are you ready for the changes you will have to make?

How flexible are you?

How flexible is your talent portfolio to making a career change?

How flexible is your resource base, i.e. social network, political network?

Are your financial resources adaptable and ready for the change?

Do you have a good support system and are they ready for the change?

Fluidity-Being able to easily change

You have adjustable skills, talents and abilities to match that of market conditions and requirements

You are financially adaptable.

You can you readily change without separating or compromising who you are, your values and your brand.

PREPARING FOR THE CHANGE

The Right Way to Lose a Job!

Knowing how to lose a job is just as important as understanding how to get one. Today's employment market requires that individuals be ready and prepared for this moment. There is fear associated with job loss but when you have the tools you need, it makes the journey less cumbersome. Your support system's stress will not be as challenging if they know you are prepared for the moment if it comes.

Now job loss is not an end goal but definitely one that you may have to journey through one day. In order to weather this storm you must be resilient, optimistic, and hopeful. In addition, you must be willing to step out on faith and to do something you've probably never done before, for example, moving to another state or region of the world in order to achieve your goals

Before you reach the job loss stage you have to be willing to change your way of thinking and start visualizing yourself accomplishing something different, something grander. Remember people don't get what they want by being lucky. It's about being prepared when an opportunity presents itself. A loss of a job is one of those opportunities. It is better to be prepared for an opportunity that may never come, than to be unprepared for the one that does come. It takes motivation, and discipline to master the unknown. Once you find out what your motivation is, you use that to give yourself the push needed to change any situation. But you also have to be disciplined in your pursuits.

If you don't have discipline, it will take longer to master your new opportunities. The personal stories I share are to help you understand Professional Freedom or How to Lose a Job the Right Way. Here goes____

Walking out of work one day, a teammate thanked me for being open and honest about not having to accept the position or the place of employment because she had choices. She went on to say that this was easy for me because I felt free to choose to stay or go. My thought at that moment was, is that not the case with everyone? I was amazed and must have outwardly demonstrated it through my facial expressions.

She hurriedly explained that if she was 20 years younger and without responsibilities that she would make a different decision about the direction of her career. She went on to speak about courage and confidence. Her comments took me back to my dissertation topic on the impact of others Psychological Capital. The night before I had a conversation with a student who had recently reviewed the study I completed on Psychological Capital. He wanted to know why I was so happy and willing to help others. He also wanted to know if I would be willing to serve on his dissertation committee. After speaking with him for a couple hours I agreed to work with him. This brings me to the culminating moment for wanting to write this book. Tonight at the business club, on the 49th floor of the 191 Building in Atlanta, Georgia, with a view of the magnificent skyline of Atlanta to the North, South East and West. A skyline that says Atlanta and the world is yours; all you have to do is capture it through what you have to offer.

We were sharing various work related stories. While sharing stories the one most pressing was the earlier story of the young lady I had walked out the office with earlier that evening. Verna's comment to me after sharing the story was "You are Free." I thought what a coincidence that I had just heard the words "You are Free" in two earlier conversations. As I shared more she mention why didn't I write about how I became so free professionally?

Individuals with Professional Freedom are secure that they have the proper sustainable balance of intellectual, social, political, and psychological capital combined with relevant talent, brand awareness and financial stability to master current and future economic conditions associated with employment market conditions. They are connected to their community and share their time, talent and treasure. They command market base prices for the services they provide. They can easily shift from one type of business to another and apply their talent offerings to increase or maintain income. They define success based on their terms and strive to master healthy levels of that success for maximum satisfaction and engagement.

Professional Freedom means having a different spectrum, filled with experiences of autonomy, , and self-sufficiency. They are qualified, proficient, and skilled. They are resilient, optimistic, and self-aware. They are fully engaged, motivated, creative, innovative and more productive workforce members. **To exist without Professional Freedom** is to live with feelings of slavery, health challenges, depression, frustrations, self-doubt, lack of adequate experience, and or lack of ability. Many of these are the characteristics and behaviors of individuals working for a paycheck or to meet responsibilities and nothing more.

In order to be a sustainable talent, you must constantly reinvent and re-educate yourself. Networking is critical for expanding your personal and professional skills, building meaningful relationships and learning new concepts and strategies that you can put into practice every day. Having a variable and changeable career means being skilled at career development and self-directed towards the goal of achieving psychological success. Individuals with professional freedom have twelve foundational components which include, intellectual, social, psychological, and political capital combined with, relevant talent, change competency, brand awareness, social responsibility, self-assessments and proper time management practices are empowered to choose current conditions or make a change. I understood these concepts from a theoretical standpoint but I did not understand the true essence of them until I was affected. I was well into writing this book when on December 13, 2011 there was a dreaded knock on my office door. One of those knocks that you know there is not so good news coming with the entrance of the person who knocked.

Your Services are No longer Needed, What!!!!

Things were awfully quiet in the office. My manager had been incognito since receiving word from her manager a few weeks ago on her new project. Over the weeks she had mentioned a few things here and there but not much had been heard from her until this afternoon when she knocked on my door. While her face was somber, she had this cruel little smirk on her face. She began the conversation by saying that she understood my sponsor for the Disability Affinity team was trying to tell me something in my previous one on one conversation with him in the prior week. That something was that I was going to be let go by this round of job cuts. She stated that I and my team were going to be laid off. She seemed to indicate that there was a possibility that I would be affected immediately. She went on to say that I should be okay out in the job market due to the fact that I had a MBA and PhD, as if that should have anything to do with this conversation.

She stayed in my office for two hours covering a lot of hearsay and other rumor mill information, then reminiscing over previous conversations related to the company's problems. She mentioned names and job eliminations of individuals that had been discussed through these rumor mills. She never specifically stated that she had factual data related to my termination, nor would I have expected her to. I let her know several times during the two hour period that I understood and that I was happy that the organization was making some decisions. I also let her know that I appreciated her taking the time to come down and let me know that I was being let go.

She informed me that there was a 30 day notice instead of a 60 day notice and that January 31st would be my last day. I thought for moment, "damn get the news during the Christmas holidays and be terminated on my birthday." She did try to soothe the news by mentioning to me several times that she thought that I should apply for some of the positions posted specifically one that she had spoken to me about a couple weeks earlier when she received news of her project from her boss.

During this two hour period various things went through my mind. First, I wanted to jump up and shake some remorse into this woman because she seemed to be celebrating my and others unfortunate challenge at hand. Second, I cautioned myself on judging myself against her and others around there. Third, I knew that I had been preparing for this moment for the last six years when she first told me to go find employment elsewhere because I did not seem to be a good fit there. Finally, I asked myself if I was going to take the advice that I had been preaching, coaching and mentoring to others since 2009, "Knowledge + Skills + Abilities +Passion =Positioning, Power, Preference and Potential" the building blocks of Professional Freedom.

I was happy when she finally stopped the small talk and left my office. Even though I had studied this and spoken about it, it was still hard to deal with the facts at hand. Financially I was not in a position to lose my twice a month pay check. Especially considering the fact that this morning I awoke to find my cable turned off. My mortgage as well as other bills was a month behind. I was now paying for my daughter's place, her college, and my son's IRS bill. I was trying to keep them out of the financial mess that I had found myself in over the years.

Yes, I knew that there was a strong possibility of this day was coming as many others in this same situation but it is just hard to actually deal with when one of the following components are missing; **Intellectual Capital** , **Social Capital, Political Capital, Psychological Capital, Relevant Talent, Personal Brand Awareness, Social Responsibility, and Financial Stability.** Currently, with debt and obligations beyond my income, I was missing financial stability. In addition, one of the areas I saw myself going was in more of an entrepreneurial or combination track, (work and business ownership). Some would call it my next step after my current gig was up.

I shut my computer down for the evening and headed to the lobby to exit the building. The guard said to me, "Have a good evening, this will all be here tomorrow."

"Will it?" I asked.

He answered with, "Why not? It always is."

My thoughts were if he only knew. Yes, he was correct in that the company and the work will always be there but it doesn't mean that the people will be. Many had left work today thinking the same, not knowing that tomorrow would be their last day at the company. They always felt that it would be there tomorrow. Some, like me, were tied to the paycheck. I had become a prostitute to a job for the money.

I reminded myself that I should know this better than most since I had spoken to her and others about this very same topic. As I admitted, you can know the truth and facts but it is hard to deal them with when you are not prepared. Later that evening, I called Claire , my best friend who also worked at the company, to make her aware of the upcoming events.

I wanted her to be strong and prepared when hearing the information from someone else and for the coming end for many of our teammates.

There are warnings for approaching bad weather, downturns in the stock market, illnesses and the list goes on. However, everyone needs to understand the challenges of change in today's business environments and how those challenges affect individual lives.

My friend and I worked together all my 17 years at the company. We had weathered many storms together and she had been my rock for many of my life challenges as I had been there for her. My friend, however, had been with the organization for over 25 years. She didn't have a degree or a backup plan. She was five years from official retirement, meaning the ability to receive a retirement check without penalty of early payment. She, like many others, was doing her best to hold on as long as possible to achieve the ultimate goal of retirement income and health coverage for lifelong service and loyalty to the organization.

Just as many who grew up during the industrial revolution, Claire believed in the Defined Benefit Plans. The loyalty model that said as long as you came to work and did the job you were asked to do and did it well, you could count on the organization to provide cost of living increases, take care of your career mapping and establish your next moves within the organization. Loyalty meant more than having an own creative and innovative voice, managing your career and being purposeful in actions around your career.

In the past I had conversations with Claire and many of my teammates on the importance of managing their careers but the thought of change was hard for them to grasp. Because that change would involve areas of their life that returning to school, attending additional training in core areas of technology enhancements or making small time management changes to provide the time needed to engage in activities around career improvements. This type of change many had moved beyond and felt was unnecessary for the next steps of their lives. Actions such as returning to school meant sitting in a classroom full of younger people and not necessarily gathering any additional knowledge around their current career goals.

That evening at dinner my idea really coalesced. It was time to take a break from the organization and test out some of the goals I had around building solutions for people who needed help with career management. I wanted to work with programmers to develop tools to use both in the workplace and personally to make managing a career an everyday process like brushing one's teeth and eating a meal for health and survival. The best approach in situations like this is to remain positive. Don't take the layoff personally because it didn't mean that I that I didn't have what it took to be successful. It just meant that my services where no longer needed for the roles I was currently filling.

I had coached friends who received offers of other positions within the organization, seemingly out of the blue, that something was about to happen in the position they currently held. These moments signaled that the organization as a whole is about to go through a change and someone who is high enough to know this is taking the time to share the information. So take heed of the advice and recommendations and be prepared for being laid off.

Preliminary Action Item:

My conversation with the manager, my sponsor and others was a warning that I may be impacted. They did not know for sure. However, their warning provided me with the opportunity to take stock. I pulled out my paper and pencil and started reviewing and updating my resume.

PFTIPS______

You should always have a resume on file and updated annually. By doing so you can respond more proactively when you receive bad news. You will be ready to make a career change and interested in considering a new opportunity. The following are few options to consider for your resume:

Discovery checklist for personal use:

First, begin the process of determining who you are? Birthdate, place of birth, where you grew up, family history, education, jobs held, travel history, technology history, significant events in life, positive events, most memorable experiences, favorite places, rules, spiritual beliefs, do you want children or have children, your family's health, your health, financial interest, community interest, social interest, current family involvement, work values, life values. This information will help you get to know yourself better.

Resume- Professional Use

Next determine what knowledge, skills and abilities you bring to the market place? Key achievements with qualitative (strong descriptions) and quantitative (numbers) information to back it up, name three to four top career strengths, key positions held for the last ten years and with qualitative (strong descriptions) and quantitative (numbers) information with outcomes including dates, position title, and company.

Other experiences including volunteer work and key talent contributions made with outcomes, writings, board participations, non-profit participation, education-highest three levels, additional schooling or work training courses which impact your talent offering, certifications, industry associations, special equipment or software expertise, speaking experience, coaching or mentoring experience that resulted in positive outcomes.

This exercise proved useful to me and others. Use the space below to get started by building a personal life history resume starting at birth? Next build a professional resume of experiences, skills, and key achievements over the last 10-15 years?

____

____

____

____

____

____

____

____

Action Item 2

At the service station the following night I saw many homeless people and thought this could be me. That if I did not play my cards right, I could need the help of the many organizations I had contributed to over the years. I needed to handle yesterday's news by strategically developing and implementing a plan to overcome my financial challenges. I wanted to stop for an adult beverage but I thought what good that would do me? Right now I needed a clear mind to map out a clear plan. This brings me to the next action item.

PFTIPS______

Based on your experiences, career moves over the years, education, talent, connections, skills, abilities and areas of passion name four to five possible career moves? A resource to help with this item is www.onet.gov. There are several tools on this site that will help you to determine possible paths based on your experience. Use the space below to complete this exercise.

____

____

____

____

____

____

____

Action Item 3

Based on my early actions in this process I decided to try to get a full-time, on-line teaching position with one of the colleges. This avenue would provide me with the opportunity to continue teaching yet provide flexibility in my schedule to run a consulting business. It would also provide me and my daughter with medical and dental benefits.

This approach would also provide me with enough income to cover my debts, mortgage, student loans, and car note. Everything else would be covered with the severance pay.

PFTIPS

Use the space below to prepare a preliminary budget, access where your money is going, how much you really need, what needs go, what can stay. Really, take some time to think about your lifestyle and what is important to you and make a plan to cover the debt that you have, living expenses for six-nine months.

___

___

___

___

___

___

___

Action Item 4

One of my plans is to look into opening my own business. A step many with my experience and age group (mid-30s –mid-to late forties) consider. This led me to work on my business plan to build a program to help others become Professionally Free.

PFTIPs __________

If you are interested in starting a business go out on *www.onet.gov* or the SBA.org to take the entrepreneurial quiz to see if this is an option you are interested in taking. If you pass the test write down some possible business ideas and over the next week come up with a business plan. Use the space below to write out your findings.

____

____

____

____

____

____

____

____

____

____

____

Over the next five weeks I continued to go to work and wait on the news of whether or not I was in the next round of cuts. I was not in the next round. It took another 60 days before I found out. While I waited for news I continued to work on the four-six steps I had outlined. I really took time to get to know myself and what I needed.

"If you ever find yourself in this situation, please take time to get know who you are and what you really want and need from your next opportunity."

I continued to attend meetings scheduled with the executive leadership of the company were I worked because this was a time to remain alert. Change was happening daily and events could change at any moment therefore gathering as much information as possible was key to my future career success.

The messages were motivating; however, I surmised that much work had to be done. Many people would need to change and still others would need letting go before the company could implement the desired strategies. In my opinion every teammate really needed to understand "who they are," "what they brought to the table," "what they knew," and "how they could best serve the organization."

Many times in situations like this new people have a better sense of the current layoff challenges than existing team members because they come in with a different perspective. Older members often don't like change and tend to protect "their" turf. This means surrounding themselves with loyal people and friends, instead of a combination of knowledgeable, creative, skilled individuals, who have innovative solutions and communication and technology skill sets needed to take the organization in the direction needed for sustainability.

How can you help to create a sustainable organization when you don't have a sustainable career?" If you don't know who you are and what skills and abilities you bring to the table, how can you play the success game with an organization trying to be successful?

I sat in meetings over the next few weeks and watched the dynamics of the room. Before becoming more knowledgeable about political posturing and organizational networking I would have seen going to such a meeting in person as an inconvenience. I would have just dialed in to the call and half listened from my desk. But now that I knew better, I understood that a big part of managing my career included understanding those who are leading the organization. This included understanding their leadership style and knowledge of their personal brand characteristics and what they stood for. I also observed new people to the organization. This was important because it provided insight on the qualities and characteristics leadership now looked for in talent.

In order to be successful in the workforce it takes a clear understanding of the characteristics those in leadership seek as part of their required talent pool. Another through brought to light while I observed the dynamics of the people in the room is competition.

What I know through research and practice is that effective productivity that brings value in the form of reduced cost and increased sales happens when people are engaged and motivated and not fearful of losing their job or competing unnecessarily. Now don't get me wrong competition is healthy when done right. However, competition on the same team is a recipe for dissatisfaction. For achievement to happen healthy competition that comes with admiration, honor and respect for those in the game helps to minimize unhealthy competition within the work environment.

I understand that those who are the most productive are individuals, who know who they are, know what they know, what they bring to the work partnership, how to blend their brand, skills, abilities, knowledge, and passion to build preference, positioning, power and potential success. Success based on your needs which are fluid in ability.

"Flow like water never changing what you are but finding a new way to get to the designation"

However, life happens and even though you have plans sometimes stumbling blocks get in the way. At these times you have to be like water and flow where the currents take you. There are going to be rocks that get in the way, just go around them. The goal is to keep flowing. Water doesn't change. The environment does and what you have to do is to change your behavior patterns and actions in order to move swiftly and not be left behind.

During the waiting period time I had a sinus infection and had to go to the doctor. The first question they asked was did I have insurance? Tears began to flow with each question— name of employer, address, who is responsible for the bill, on and on the questions, went. Questions I had never thought much about. She then said the bill would be $50.00 for the visit and must be paid before the doctor can see you. She must have thought that I was in severe pain the way the tears where flowing. The pain was not as bad as the moment of possible truth in knowing that I may not be able to answer those questions and pay that bill if I didn't move swiftly in my thoughts and actions. That this type of normal life event could be a challenge in the future. Paying a bill had not been a worry of mine since working in the current industry, which started 22 years ago.

My experience at the facility was flawless, despite being upset over the co-pay of $50.00. By the end of the visit I felt like a new person. Without insurance this visit, plus the medication could have cost me in excess of $2,500 hundred dollars. That was something to think about. I left there and called my manager, I took my first sick day in five years. It was simply too late in the day to go to work.

Bad habits must cease

In the past I may have forgotten to pay some bill because I had a lot on my mind or because I was busy taking care of others business. This was something that needed to change.

PFTIPS______

Make a list of bad habits that would need to change regardless of the news.

____

____

____

____

____

____

____

Some things included communicating with those I help to support this included my son and daughter. The reason my son needed my help was because he had made mistakes with his taxes and had not planned properly. In addition to all of this happening my daughter who had received a conditional job offer had leased an apartment that I was paying the expenses for until the job came through which was to happen a couple months earlier. I also paid my daughters expenses for college.

PFTIPS______

Make a list and talking points of items you need to discuss. Think about how you would like to structure the conversations. Change for me meant changes for everyone relying and depending on my income; including the non-profits I contributed to so religiously.

____

____

____

Action Item 5

Make a budget of your current expenses

- Decide on what you can live with
- It is estimated that it will take 80% of current income to continue your current standard of living
- Only spend 4% of your 401(k) income the first year.
- Decide if you are the type that needs a monthly check (annuity payments)
- Or if you truly believe you can manage the money yourself you may want a lump sum payment option

Action Item 6:

Understand the tax consequences of your retirement distribution decisions.

PFTIPS______

- Lump sum payments will incur a 20% immediate tax withholding and an additional 10% penalty tax if you are not at least 59 ½ on distribution date
- If you have stock in your retirement plan check on NUA if you plan to take the stock distribution in-kind
- If you have loans in the 401(k) plan, check on what options you have available in some cases you only have two options; (1) Don't pay the loan and receive a 1099. You will have to pay taxes on the amount withdrawn of 20% and 10% penalty tax. (2) Repay the loan

____

____

____

____

____

____

____

____

____

MASTERING THE LAYOFF

February 27, 2012

I woke up at 2am, as sick as I could be. My head was spinning and I could not hear out of my left ear. In addition, two months and 2 weeks after my first warning that a possible notice was coming, I receive the final answer on my employment status with the company received news today that my position was no longer needed due to the reorganization of responsibilities to various teams within the company. While I agree that a new business model was needed, it meant that changes in my personal life needed to occur.

When I received the news that March 31, 2012 would be my last day, I knew that I had to have a plan of action in place for the next 32 days. My office at the end of the day was surrounded with people receiving the same news and others. My voicemail was packed and cell phones were ringing and receiving text after text. All from people wanting to know what my plans were. So I decided to complete a blog my actions and Professional Freedom Tips for the next 30 days through the March 31, 2012 date.

My son texted me and asked me to leave his mail and the tickets to an event on the counter. I texted back and said that I would. I also let him know that we would need to renegotiate his payments to the IRS because my last day at work would be March 31st. I hated to have to tell my son this. Tears came to my eyes.

The one thing that parents hate to do is disappoint their kids especially when they know that their kids really need them. My son picked up the phone concerned and asked if I was okay. I let him know everything that had been going on, from the lay off to the current sinus infection. I told him that everything would be okay but for the first time I felt he didn't believe me. He was concern because he knew how hard it would be to replace a six figure salary. Even though I worked part-time teaching college, those earnings were dedicated to repaying my student loan debt. This was a goal I made for myself while attending college and one way I believed that I could continue to learn and give back to the collegiate community at the same time.

Day 1

I decided to have lunch at the Business Club I belonged to and enjoy this moment overlooking the city of Atlanta at the club where I came up with the idea for this book earlier the year before. I had not been able to finish the book because it was missing something which I soon came to realize was my current impending termination announcement. After picking up my daughter and settling in for lunch at the club. I shared with my daughter the news. Immediately she said this may be a good thing. "*As you have stated, to me as well as to Alex and I, that change is good. You can do so much more and you shouldn't have a problem getting another job or doing your own thing. You have prepared yourself for whatever happens. At any rate you seem to know how to survive. You have proven this time and time again. Again, some kind of way you survive, you always have and you have taught us to do the same.*"

Her comments to me were priceless!! At twenty she was so mature and so much likes her mother and grandmother. That day, I was the proudest mother. I had raised two children, who weren't selfish and who had a moral and responsible conscious. Even through all the hours of work and sacrifices their faith in me served as a reminder that all the schooling, work, and late nights with little to no sleep was worth it. Before, I was thinking how much I hated disappointing them but I hadn't. They knew, just as I did, that it was time to leave my job and this was the push I needed to try something different. Just as many other older workers, who know they have stayed in their present job for too long, I had become complacent due to being tied to a paycheck and to personal responsibilities.

I really enjoyed my afternoon with my daughter. It was great to have time to sit down and have a conversation and laugh with her. All too soon, it was now time to leave for my part-time gig. I needed to go to the school where I had teaching assignments to finish grading papers as well as other materials to review for the end of the quarter.

That night, I went to bed at peace knowing that I had the support of those closest to me. The following are helpful Personal Freedom Tips to consider.

PFTIPS______

- Communicate immediately with your family. This is a great time to pull out those practice conversations notes discussed earlier.
- Establish the order of discussions and start the process. Speak positively and with your preliminary plan of action. Your network will not worry as much if they know that you have a plan in place.
- Make sure you include the following in your conversations: What happen, Why, Your plans, and What if anything you need from them. Is it best to establish this going in even though you will make changes along the way?

____

____

____

____

____

____

____

____

____

____

____

____

Day 2

I awoke this morning at 6am and began my day. I turned on CNN on one TV and CNBC on another. This was a daily routine I went through to help me stay on top current event for both work and teaching business classes. Understanding current events is crucial especially if you are a subject matter expert. For local news I subscribed to the Atlanta Journal Constitution and the Wall Street Journal online. I turned on my computer while eating breakfast and listening to the news and completed my tweet for the day. I had not tweeted for a couple of days due to everything that had happened. Once I tweeted I checked all my emails starting with the Bank, the three schools I was contracted to teach for this quarter, then my personal website, LinkedIn, Facebook, Gmail and AOL.

I made phone calls to line up a full-time job with benefits by end of March 2012. I only had four weeks to accomplish this task. My first call was to a friend from graduate school who was a manager at an online school. In addition, I contacted a public relations person for help in launching my career management certification program for individuals. I had spoken to her earlier in the week and promise to provide her with some materials she needed in order to assist me.

Lastly, I had a conference call with Social Security Administration geared towards helping individuals suffering from a disability in rejoining the workforce. Next, I had promised a friend that I would connect with an executive at a local hospital to vet their new invention and set up a breakfast or lunch meeting. Finally, I had a dinner appointment with one of my girlfriends at the business club at 6pm.

PFTIPS______

- Start charting your activity to see how you typically spend your time. Effective time management skills will become even more important due to the impending change.
- Start the planning process and implement your preliminary findings discussed earlier. Start with those connections that can possibly help you land your chosen opportunity immediately.
- Who are they and how do they fit into your short term goal?

____

____

____

____

____

____

____

____

Day 3

As my life begins to unfold in writing even I am exhausted with everything I am doing. However, for the most part I am having fun even in the midst of this chaos. I believe this is because I have a life outside of my work. I volunteer within the community, serve on non-profit boards and have connected with many contacts that make a significant difference for me and those I serve. I have positioned myself with many of the components of Professional Freedom. This included additional knowledge in leadership and how leaders of large corporations go through the decision making process. I also enhanced my skills in social and political capital. I increased my brand awareness in the community, and greatly increased my goals around being accountable and relevant in social responsibility by giving my time, talent and treasure.

***PFTIPS*______**

This is not the time to have a pity party. If you have been doing your work and looking introspectively at your talents and the opportunities available to you, proceed with confidence. Pity, sadness and misery puts you further behind your timeline in achieving your goals.

Think of the positive and focus on the positives this new opportunity affords you with. Begin by listing the positives and opportunities below:

____

____

Day 4

Now that I have to find private health insurance, health issues add to the cost equation. I begin my day with a workout, something I should have taken into serious consideration before today. I watched the news, CNN, CNBC, and Fox news during my workout. Once I finished my workout, I started working on my agenda items for today which included: updating my Twitter account, spending time with my children and grandchildren, writing and submitting applications for three full-time online teaching positions. I also decided to apply for a couple of Dean of Business positions just in case.

Later I joined my family for some quality time. This was also a chance to discuss the changes that were taking place. Sitting there talking with my kids, I realized how many stakeholders where potentially affected by my six figure income loss. Most certainly my family and friends were affected, but so were local businesses that I frequented, like my hairdresser, pedicure and manicurists, masseuse, grocery store, pharmacist. It wasn't just local businesses. Large corporations like Macys, Dillard's, ATT, Bank of America, Chase, SunTrust, Business Club, Curb Market, Starbucks, Georgia Power, Federal Student Loans, Shell, Citgo, QT, would feel the loss of my patronage. However the most bitter and depressing for me were the non-profits I supported-- United Way, Georgia Appointed Court Advocates, Georgia Business Leadership Network, ABC Elite Foundation, and Church.

- I shared these names to show the impact of just one consumer being laid off. Now, just imagine that number times millions? We all share responsibility in the economic challenges we are experiencing by not being prepared with the tools needed to be relevant and sustainable in an uncertain economically challenged world of business and work. My goals for today included: Finding health Insurance for future needs, Second, make a connection with the new Dean at one of the schools I serve as an Adjunct Professor to seek help in landing full-time employment and advice on launching a new service to the school. Third goal, ensure that I spend time with team impacted to help with anything they may need. Forth goal, spend time reviewing and connecting with my inner self ensure peace with my new life opportunity and thanking God each day for his blessing.

***PFTIPS*______**

Start your day with your number one goal in mind.

- Find Health Insurance?
- Second goal make a connection with a potential employer or contact someone who can connect you with a potential employer.

- Third goal, spend time reviewing and connecting with my inner self ensure peace with my new life opportunity and thanking God each day for his blessing.

Day-5

Health and Dental Insurance and notifying personal contacts

PFTIPS______

- Remain positive, always look on the upside, anger will get you nowhere, it slows down the process
- Find health insurance- If you need to replace health insurance because of your Reduction in Force notice (RIF's) opportunity, you will need to start this process in order to have insurance in place on day one. Check out www.Einsurance.com
- Add to the list of those you want to stay connected with and the reason why: Trust me this will be important later
- If possible make a connection with a future employment prospect
- Make a list of all the charities you support and establish what you will be able to offer them during your transition period. Now is a good time to offer more time in your key areas of expertise it will help you gain additional experience.
- Have drinks or dinner with possible connections
- Before you contact anyone outside of your immediate family write a 30 second pitch about what just happen for example: "Hello Sally, today I received notice that my position was being eliminated. I wanted to thank you for your support and ask that you continue

that support. Sally, I ask that you see this as a positive move and that you take some time over the next few weeks in helping me to brainstorm some ideas around my future. Thanks for your positive words of encouragement."

Day 6-

Look at the Positive

"Man's greatness lies in the power of thought." Blasé Pascal

***PFTIPS*______**

- Accept the news, it's nothing personal.
- Review your Reduction In Force, (RIF) package, make notes
- Make a list of all projects and your work responsibilities
- Work with your current employer to ensure that you hand off items properly and effectively. When you start your new life you want need distractions. Ensure that you end your contract professionally.
- Don't spend time worrying about the past. Look forward to the future
- Have a celebration with those closes to you on your new opportunity.
- Discuss possibilities while celebrating your blessing.
- Write down 3-5 possible networking connections
- Get a notebook and write down what you liked most and didn't like about your current position (You will add to this notebook so keep it by your side)

Day 7-

Review Income and Expenses

It's a small world. Trust me globalization and technology make it easy to reconnect with the same people in a different place so remain professional at all times.

PFTIPS_______

- Continue working with your current employer to ensure that you had off items properly and effectively. When you start your new life you will not need distractions.
- Ensure that you end your contract professionally. Remain positive, always looking on the upside, anger will get you nowhere, it slows down the process
- Spend time reading through your RIF package for understanding, make notes of who to contact
- Create an Income and Expense Statement/budget – What do you need to maintain your current lifestyle? What is realistic based on income and investments on hand? Finally, what can you live with?
- This may be a good time to contact a financial planner. If you don't have one, based on your income and expenses, you may need expert advice. It may pay for itself in the long run.
- List unnecessary expenses to cut

- Complete a preliminary tax return to review what your tax situation may look like, if you have an accountant contact him/her
- Establish a timeline covering personal tasks which must be covered, i.e. Doctors and Dentist appointments, eye exams
- List out your values- For example, I value my mornings so in my next position I ideally would need like to start my work day around 10am-11am. Now my day starts at 5am but I need personal time before heading out.
- Pull out your resume-review and update with most relevant data. If the organization provides outplacement services they will work with you on how to structure properly.
- Make an appointment with outplacement services if provided
- Continue adding to your list of things you liked and didn't like about your current position
- Write down a possible career you have always wanted to try?

____

____

____

____

____

____

Day-8

Life Insurance and Retirement Plans

Understand the current options of transferring your life insurance if it is through your employer; if you can't whether due to cost or other find a replacement – again seek the help of a financial planner if needed.

***PFTIPS*______**

- Review your retirement plan options- seek the help of a financial planner if needed
- Remain positive, always looking on the upside, anger will get you nowhere, it slows down the process
- Add to the list of those you want to stay connected with and the reason why: Trust me this will be important later
- If possible make a connection with a future employment prospect
- Continue adding to your list of things you liked and didn't like about your current position
- Continue adding to careers you have always wanted to try?
- Make a lunch connection date
- Start packing your office
- Establish a timeline with your employer for handing off major responsibilities
- Write down 3-5 possible networking connections

- Do something to relax, play music, enjoy a concert enjoy!!

Day-9

Self-Knowledge

"Have faith in God, "Jesus answered. (23)I tell you the truth, if anyone says to this mountain, Go, throw yourself into the sea, and does not doubt in his heart but believes that what he says will happen, it will be done for him. (24) Therefore I tell you, whatever you ask for in prayer, believe that you have received it, and it will be yours." (Mark 11:22-24)

The news received this week can be seen as positive or negatively. I choose positive. I see this as a time to reflect and ask God to reveal his direction for your life. In my case, I believe that he was preparing me for my next journey seven years prior when I was provided with the vision to return to school. That direction provided me with the internal strength to know that this was not the end but the beginning of something wonderful and fabulous. I know this something will bring me one step closer to the vision for my life's purpose. Therefore, my direction starts with having faith that, even though I had become comfortable working for my current employer for 17 years, I was now mature and strong enough in my vision, knowledge, skills, abilities, and talents to move in a new direction.

PFTIPS______

- Equipped with the knowledge of the first eight days use today to reflect on the list you have made to date and start writing down your areas of strengths, your vision for your future, knowledge you have obtained to date, skills, abilities, and talents. (Talents are those things you do well without having the necessary educational knowledge or training)

- Add to the list of those you want to stay connected with and the reason why: Trust me this will be important later
- If possible make a connection with a future employment prospect
- Continue adding to your list of things you liked and didn't like about your current position
- Continue adding to careers you have always wanted to try?
- Write down 3-5 possible networking connections

____

____

____

____

____

____

____

____

____

____

____

Day-10

Take Action Day

As I have stated throughout the last nine days, I found it important to connect each day with at least one potential employer or client. Throughout my post over this thirty day period I will use employer and client interchangeably. Why? Because, we all really work for ourselves, some assignments are long-term and others are short-term based on the need of the client as well as your individual needs.

Out of the list of possible contacts for employer/client put them in the order of significance to you. Significance could mean those that you want to connect with for interviewing experience or that you see your knowledge, skills, and abilities adding value to.

***PFTIPS*______**

- If possible make a connection with a future employment prospect continue adding to careers you have always wanted to try?
- Write down 3-5 possible networking connections
- Write down those things you received praises for from your current employer, client, teammates, or others
- Ask teammates to link to you or you them on LinkedIn. In addition ask some from different areas to provide you with a recommendation. Make sure that recommendations highlight your

strengths and abilities. These should complement the areas you wish to provide services to in your future

- If possible meet with a future employment prospect, this should be one of the individuals you connected with earlier. Make sure you ask for what you want. Even if they can't help you, they may know someone who can
- Do something to relax, go to a movie, enjoy a play, take a long weekend trip

Day-11

Day to Reflect

I start each day reading the Bible. I think that it was divine intervention that this was a goal I established at the beginning of the year. This has truly made a significant impact on my actions this week. After my daily reading I prayed and asked God to provide direction on the list and actions I had put together for the last eleven days. Situations are truly what you make of them. Your thoughts and actions have a significant impact on how you arrive at your future. I am a positive person and choose to be happy with things that are presented to me.

***PFTIPS*______**

- Spend 30 minutes connecting spiritually, and being thankful for your journeys in life yes, evening the one you are about to embark on.
- Work four hours on your plan including establishing plans for the following week (a) developing a draft of your resume (b) develop a contact list for the following week along with why you wish to connect (c) build a checklist for the following week including items to take care at the office, (d) make a list of appointments outstanding
- Spend 30 minutes to an hour exercising or start a program if you haven't already

- Check on banking account information to ensure that you have the best deal possible
- Do something to relax

Day-12

Day of Rest

Relax today, have fun and enjoy family and friends

- Remain positive, always looking on the upside. Anger will get you nowhere, it slows down the process

Day 13–

Believe in Self- Voice It, Ask for It, Claim It, and Accept It

It takes commitment, motivation, and persistence for an individual to reach a new plateau in life. Day 13 was very exciting for me. I met with one of my contacts whom I had not had the privilege before of a one on one conversation. My hour with her was invaluable. I knew that this individual had connections and political power but I was not aware of her knowledge, innovative and visionary acuity. After my meeting with her, one of the contacts I had reached out to over the weekend called me back, I shared with him what I was looking for and he asked me to email him my most recent resume. I forwarded it from my iPhone and received a call five hours later from one of his colleagues with a job offer.

This brings me to this point. When you want to achieve more, simply make the effort to achieve the desired goals. I have many goals; therefore I must stay focused and aim for the targets that this RIF notice has afforded me the opportunity to approach.

The motivation behind the goal is the fuel that ignites the desire. Along with the offer I received, I also connected with a friend to see how we could work together on a potential consulting contract. My final connection was with the outplacement service. I started the process of entering my profile information into their job center. This experience was great because

I found that something I had been working on was already available. So this may change my focus for a current business project I am launching.

***PFTIPS*_______**

The following website www.mappingyourfurture.org provides some valuable information on how to understand possible directions you would like take your career. The process starts by assessing your interest and determining what it is that you like to do. This is because the direction you decide to take has a significant impact on your life. The site suggests that you make note some of the following; the importance of knowing what you like doing as well as reflecting on experiences you have enjoyed.

Next the site ask you to make a list of 10 activities you have enjoyed doing in the past four years. This is insightful, because when you look back there should be some connection to why you were involved in these activities. What challenges did the activities offer? What skills do you need to develop further to continue in those activities? All of these questions can help you to evaluate your next career path.

- Remain positive, always looking on the upside, anger will get you nowhere, it slows down the process
- Check out www.mappingyourfurture.org
- Make a list of 10 activities you have enjoyed doing in the past four years
- What challenges did the activities offer

- What skills do you need to develop further to continue in those activities
- Make sure that you have copies on your last three years reviews
- Think about any projects you participated in and the role you played, write down your accomplishments
- Make a contact to a decision maker and let him/her know what your position is and your goal

Day 14

My Choice- Job, Career, or Passion

Mortimer J. Adler an American philosopher and educator once quoted the following which I find so appropriate.

"Every idea is a source of life and light which animates and illuminates the words, facts, examples, and emotions that are dead or deadly and dark without them. Not to engage in this pursuit of ideas is to live like ants instead of like men."

When I arrived at the office I had an email from a lady I had met at a Professional Women's event last evening. During our conversations that evening she had asked me about possible books she should read. I recommended about 12 books including two I had written as good reads. To my surprise she quoted information from my first book, "Antidotal Poetry for Career and Professional Success".

This reminded me that I needed to ensure that my next step was one of the three. In addition, this morning's daily spiritual reading and lesson came from Numbers and Mark. The lesson learned for me is that anyone can give who has it to give; just as anyone can work a job if they have the talents to work it. If you have maintained a career before, great you can do that again but it takes faith, perseverance and determination to follow your passion. Therefore, even with job offer in hand, I am strongly considering pursuing my business opportunity as well.

My opportunity is now. What about you?

PFTIPS______

Review list or complete list from the previous day

- Make a list of 10 activities you have enjoyed doing in the past four years
- What challenges did the activities offer
- What skills do you need to develop further to continue in those activities
- Make sure that you have copies of your last three years reviews
- Think about any projects you participated in and the role you played, write down your accomplishments
- Make a contact to a decision maker and let him/her know what your position is and your goal

____

____

____

____

____

____

____

____

Day 16

Take Nothing for Granted-Doors will open

"The forms of Virtue are: justice, courage, magnificence, magnanimity, liberality, gentleness, prudence, wisdom." Aristotle (384-322) Greek Philosopher

I worked from home, took meetings and read emails, but in between those times I took care of as many things as possible. I had another great day. After several meetings and connections I was presented with an opportunity to speak at an upcoming Women's Leadership conference next month. This would present me with the opportunity to add to my list of speaking engagements. I could market my company as well as seize the opportunity to connect with some great women leaders from around the country.

The topic related well with my company's mission and goals. The universe was lining up. For the most part people had been wonderful and ready to assist in whatever aspect possible. I truly believed that the doors I had seen opened are due to the amount of time I spent giving of my time, talent, and treasure freely without conditions being tied to it. My actions helped me to build a network of individuals aware of my talent offerings and my character.

"Know what you know and what you do not know, consistently ask questions and seek the truth for those things which could lead to roadmaps for success. Never stop learning or

growing. Knowledge is wisdom, wisdom is power that doesn't cost a dime but without it the cost can be outrageous." Marilyn Carroll

I thank God for all the wonderful individuals he has placed in my life's path whether it is for a reason, season, or purpose. I am truly grateful. I will provide times so that you can use them as examples.

I signed off the work site at 5:00 pm, then worked another 4 hours on the following tasks:

PFTIPS______

- Write Thank You notes to connections you spoke with last week Make Dentist appointment
- Purchase personal business cards with name, phone number, emails address include positive messaging on back of card if desired otherwise leave professional. These come in handy when networking.
- Set up an appointment to meet with a Career Coach provided by outplacement service.
- Continue to build resume information

____

____

____

____

____

Day 17

Pushed Over the Edge

I woke up excited about my new direction. I truly believed that a seed had been planted in me that will help many people struggling in careers or aiming to make decisions about possible career directions. Praying without ceasing for direction and guidance, I needed strength to make the right decisions about the business I received the vision to accomplish. The layoff for just the push over the edge of the cliff I needed. This brings me to a point I need to make.

Okay, to all of you who have never been RIF, or downsized here is a message for you. "*Please stop saying to people that you are sorry to hear their news unless their news really impacts you in some way.*" Try this. "*Please let me know if there is anything I can do for you once you get settle. I will you send my contact information.*" Or "*I am on LinkedIn I would be happy to recommend you based on our working relationship together.*"

The day started early because I had to make it to the office early to cover for the other managers who would not be in until later. They had touched base with me the night before to let me know that they would be in later. Upon my arrival to the office I saw several co-workers had left messages that they would like to connect. Each asked me how was I doing and what I planned to do. I provided them with my prepared 30 to 60 second marketing pitch about my next steps. (You need this if you don't already have one. And it needs to be so contagious that others are excited want to join you).

It was a busy day. I had several conference calls on my list for and one lunch meeting. Unexpectedly, I received a call from a Provost of a school inquiring about my possible interest in teaching. I would say that I have been lucky; however, luck only comes to those prepared. I had prepared for many possible directions over the last few years.

Remember this for the day, people with good intentions will be full of well wishes, you have many things to accomplish. Don't waste time, because time is not your friend. Complete as many things as possible. Remain positive and complete items on your list. If you have not contacted the outplacement service, try to do so no later than the next business day. Do you need a Push? Are you experiencing Your Time? Nothing is as powerful as an idea or action whose time has come.

***PFTIPS*______**

- Develop a spreadsheet with contact information with those at work and within my work email list
- Send emails to email subscription providers on periodicals and newsletters to let them know of my new email address
- Build a spreadsheet of those within the organization to have lunch or dinner with while I was fresh on their minds

- Clear out another set of file drawers and send information to appropriate individuals (4 file drawers remain) my goal was two per day

Day 18

Good Decision Making is Key

My manager requested that the Retirement Education Specialist's provide a general overview of our retirement, health and welfare options for those interested. The Specialist stressed the importance of good decision making as it relates to retirement decisions. Now many of us in the room had been in Employee Benefits Administration for an average of 20 years but when something gets closer to home and directly impacts you it becomes more important to sit in the learning seat.

Do you understand the decision you are about to make? Do you have what you need to make an intelligent decision?

***PFTIPS*______**

Know your retirement income sources

- Company's retirement Plan
- Company's 401(k) Plan
- Social Security
- Retirement Income from other sources
- IRA's
- Personal savings and investments
- Home equity and real estate

- Residual income from royalties, rent, speaking, tapes, or other sources

Health and Life Insurance

- Ensure that you understand your rights under Cobra as well as other options available. As stated in an earlier post check out e insurance for some good rates and quotes
- Review current life insurance policies ensure that your goal for originally selecting the policy is the same today

Day 19:

Lets' Move Mountains

Let's face it we don't need a lot to live off. We have made our life complicated by those things that we see and hear. We want because we believe that there is nothing we can't have. That's fine but the job market is a beast. In order to conquer any beast it is important that you be prepared and make wise decisions.

Due to advancements in technology, globalization and knowledge in addition to increased education, today's work environment is more competitive than ever before. We are competing with job seekers from around the world. The country is more diverse than ever which brings about a whole new generation of people with various skill sets. Once again, competition for jobs is fierce.

People who are great at what they do are out of work. Even if you can't land a job with a company, you may have to consider using your innate talents and abilities to gain economic empowerment. For example, the guy that started 1 800 JUNK used an old truck to start a business that went on to be a million dollar ideal. He used his innate abilities around junk and trash removal to propel him to riches. Each of us has some great thought and/or action plan that can produce revenue for us. You have to think about what that is for you.

Don't be afraid. This is your time of opportunity. Take hold and "work the plan and don't let the plan work you."

***PFTIPS*______**

- What innate talents and abilities can you possibly capitalize on?
- Check your list of lunch, dinner and drinks dates, you are two weeks away from your last day
- Prepare letters for three potential employers or add to your list of possible connections of future employment prospects
- Continue adding to your list of things you liked and didn't like about your current position
- Continue adding to careers you have always wanted to try?
- Write down 3-5 possible networking connections

____

____

____

____

____

____

____

____

Day 20

Reflect and renew – You have wings, fly!

I received the following email from an individual in my social network, "Marilyn, thanks for letting me know the news. I am thinking about you and wish you the very best in your new endeavors." Perfect!!! This is another example of how to communicate with someone who has been laid off People who are impacted don't want pity. They want actions that will help them move on to their next steps in their career journey.

In order to be a sustainable talent, you must constantly reinvent and re-educate yourself. Networking is critical for expanding your personal and professional skills, building meaningful relationships and learning new concepts and strategies that you can put into practice every day.

I see the lay off as an opportunity. Even if I am afraid of the hidden obstacles in my next journey in life, I believe that I can accomplish the opportunity presented before me. I have wings to approach my next destination along with faith that my new journey was ordained. In order to achieve my desired goal of helping others, I must be willing to do something I have never done before, change from that which is comfortable.

I have to be willing to change my way of thinking and start visualizing myself accomplishing my goal. This is not luck nor is it misfortune but faith through works and knowledge which have lead me to this place of opportunity. My seventeen years of service and acquired education, knowledge, and experience have prepared me for when an opportunity presents itself. This time is the time of opportunity.

It takes motivation, and discipline to achieve desired goals. Since I know my motivation is to help others become economically empowered, I will use that to give me the drive I need to master my current situation.

However, I understand that discipline is optimum to achieving my pursuits; therefore maintaining focus with my actions, times and resources are keys to successfully meeting or exceeding my goals.

***PFTIPS*______**

If you have not landed employment, do the following:

Start a notebook with the following information:

- Paint a picture of how you see yourself in the future. Use existing artwork or magazines.
- Establish a word list of action words which describe you
- Establish a list of values which are important to you. For example I like a flexible work schedule. Or I like a company that values pets and parts of their employees' family.
- List out your strengths
- List out your innate abilities
- List your most admirable quality

Day 21:

The Will to Succeed

I received the following email from a friend in my network who had found out the day before that I was RIF'd. *"I am sorry to hear that you are being laid off! That's horrible. I really thought that the banking sector had stabilized, however I guess this was not the case at all. Well, I guess this frees you up to do something else you really wanted to do. Hope you find something to throw yourself into! Whatever it is I am sure that you will succeed in it because you really have a "go out there and get it" personality and those guys always seem to win!"*

His greeting acknowledges my possible hardship but he also acknowledges that it could be a blessing. He comes back with something positive. This is acceptable. So, should I take the job track and work for another company, school, or organization? Or should I take the entrepreneurial track and work on something I am passionate about and that I have been provided the vision for or a combination of both? I have worked, reviewed and analyzed all three the past 22 days.

<u>Sampling of Work Track Considerations</u>

I had to look in my talent closet to see what resources I had available to help me move to next steps (My Innate abilities, plus my acquired abilities). To ensure that I make the most appropriate decision, I posted for another job and received a call for a three phone interviews. One company wanted to get me into their finalists list if it all worked out but first I had to pass through the first three interviewers.

All went well and I was scheduled for the next phase involving a panel. One of the questions asked by all three was if I was willing to relocate. Now listen up everyone looking for a job. You need to know the answer to this question before you are asked. In addition you should know if your current location is conducive to employment opportunities in the field you have chosen or are interested in pursuing.

Sampling of Entrepreneurial Track Considerations

In order to replace my income there is a high possibility that I may have to move or travel extensively. I also realize the impact of a move on my current lifestyle. However, all options must be on the table before I can make an educated decision around acceptance of any position. Again, my first preference is to start and run my own company which is geared towards helping people. In doing so, a certain amount of capital is needed for the first two years to run the company in manner which will yield the type of return to investors as well as clients and other stakeholders.

Therefore, my options are many but I will need to make a final decision within the next 7days.

My task list for today is to continue updating the notebook started on yesterday keeping in mind the following list.

***PFTIPS*______**

- Remain positive, always looking on the upside, anger will get you nowhere, it slows down the process
- Paint a picture of how you see yourself in the future. Use existing artwork or magazines.
- Establish a word list of action words which describe you
- Establish a list of values which are important to you. For example I like a flexible work schedule. Or I like a company that values pets and sees them as part of their employees' family.
- List out your strengths
- List out your innate abilities
- List your most admirable quality

Day 22:

Your Personal Brand

Personal branding is a personal marketing and advertisement process used to establish with your audience who you are (personal) and what you do (career) and how successful you are at what you do. Today, I had lunch with an associate. We spoke about personal branding and ensuring that we establish and maintain our brand. Always allowing our audience to identify who we are and what we are about. She wanted to make sure that, whatever direction I decided to go in, I personify my personal brand.

As a continuous learner, I could identify with some of her statements. I am always interested in relevant thought that is backed up by evidence and research. In this case I am aware that there are times when I want to relax, not wear my hair a certain way, totally change my style, not wear makeup and the list goes on. I never realized the number of people who pay so much attention to how you dress, the type of car you drive, the way you wear your hair, down to the shoes on your feet. I decided to research the topic also to see what others believed about personal brand. In researching the topic I found the following article; "The Brand Called You," written by Tom Peters http://www.fastcompany.com/magazine/10/brandyou.html. Mr. Peters discusses in this article that a brand is not only the items I mentioned above but more so what you do in your career, how you perform the roles required of that career. Please read the article to get a better grasp the concepts surrounding personal branding.

My tasks today involved separating items into categories while remaining positive about the outcomes. One friend has set up meetings with possible connections on both the business and work side.

PFTIPS______

In a few words describe your brand. Your brand is how you want others to see you and want them to think about when they see you.

___

___

___

___

___

___

___

___

___

___

___

___

___

Day 23:

Still not sure of where you are going?

I have 6 days left in this process. Before I make my final decision I went through a series of questions each day.

PFTIPS______

The following questions help you to evaluate your career path:

- Do you know what you value the most?
- What are you looking for in your next career path? Do you understand what direction you would like take your career?
- Have you evaluated what your interests are and determined what it is that you like to do?
- Are you considering a path because you feel that it is safe? Have you considered similar job paths that may be unfamiliar or a job that you could do, but never before considered?
- Have you thought about experiences you have enjoyed?
- Can you name 5 activities you have enjoyed doing in the past four years?
- Do you have the knowledge, skills and abilities required to be an expert at something you are passionate about?
- Do you have an up-to-date resume?

Day 24:

The right connections are important.

Today is the day to reflect and review on your social capital.

PFTIPS______

- Do you have a solid social network?
- Do you understand the importance of social media, especially LinkedIn and the personal info and references/referrals?
- Are you aware of sites like LinkedIn/Monster etc...to use for job recommendations to expand the search from what you think applies to you to what is recommended?
- You might identify an opportunity otherwise overlooked, have you?
- Do you have the name of a good recruiter?

____

____

____

____

____

____

____

____

Day 25:

Intellectual Capital and Innate Skills

Human Capital–I assessed my intellectual and human capital components. Even though I made my decision, it is good to understand what got me here and that what got me here want keep me here unless I am prepared for the next move.

***PFTIPS*______**

Evaluate your Talent, Skills, and Abilities

- Do you understand the importance of certifications and credentials for your chosen career area of focus?
- Are your skills up to date? If not what do you need?
- Are you technology challenged?
- Do you use tools such as smart phones, Tablets and other devices frequently?
- Are you diverse in working with individuals, situations, systems?

____

____

____

____

____

____

____

____

____

Day 26:

Psychological Capital

I realize that the level of hope, optimism, resiliency and self-efficacy (self-knowledge) I have will impact my ability to weather the possible many challenges I may face over the next few years. Building a business is not easy. Starting something new is not easy. Combining both is even more difficult. I have made choices that I must be prepared to handle. The following are questions I asked myself.

PFTIPS______

- Do you know yourself? (Self-efficacy)
- When you think of yourself what words come to mind?
- When others think of you what words come to mind? (Your Brand)
- Are you hopeful about the future? (Hope)
- Are you optimistic about moving into your next step in your career? (Optimistic)
- Can you bounce back from uncertainty? (Resilience)
- Can you cope with failure? (Resilience)

___

___

___

Day 27:

Financial Capital Review

I had an appointment with my financial advisor and attorney to review decisions to ensure that I had not overlooked anything. These visits allowed me to take another look at my finances and the decisions I would need to make regarding my retirement and termination pay. I completed preliminary tax returns to review with financial advisor. This information also provided me with a view of what I had to plan for in both future work and business.

***PFTIPS*________**

- How important is pay and benefits?
- All else equal is money a determining factor in your career transition decision?
- Can you survive off of less?
- Can you relocate? If so at your cost?
- What monetary requirements will your new role call for?
- How much capital reserve do you have?
- How many months of reserve are required?
- How is your credit?
- If you had to, how long can you live off of less?

Day 28:

One door closes and another one opens

This is my last day at company where I have spent the last 17 years of my life. A new chapter begins.

This was my last day, March 29th in the office. Over the last 15 days I applied for seven positions as well as working on the launch of my company, KSAP5i. The reason for applying for these positions was to ensure that I had enough revenue coming in to pay for the business without seeking additional financial assistance. As well as allowing me to continue to contribute to another area of business which I am passionate about career management education. Other benefits include: flexibility, benefits, and the ability to continue to increase my knowledge while giving back and helping others.

Of the positions I applied for two were with the current organization. In both positions I would be performing roles I felt confident I would excel. One of the positions was filled with another in house candidate and the other as of my exit from the company was not announced. The other five positions were external to the organization. I was offered all five.

I made the decision to go with the position which would provide me with the most opportunities as well as compliment my business. The position required travel but that did not bother me. I was very open to doing what I needed to do to be successful as long as it meant that I would not have to compromise on what I valued, my passion, or my goals.

Day 29:

Values and Decision Making

How do you know that you are making the best decision possible? Rule of thumb is this. Key decisions require that you receive all the relevant information possible from various reliable sources. First you must check the information they provided across another source. Second, check with outside sources including as I mentioned earlier in this series of post a financial advisors. Finally, evaluate and analyze all the information. Compare this information with your current and future goals.

Day 30:

ARE YOU READY? I AM!!

Ending a 17 year career contract for a new beginning and the possibilities are endless!

Knowledge +Skills+Abilities+Passion=Potential+Positioning+Preference+Power=Individual Plan **(KSAP5i)**

Some change must occur in order for growth to happen. The greater the change the more the growth, leading to exponential opportunities. So have faith, build on hope, live in courage, and be optimistic about the future.

I start my new role on Monday, April 2, 2012. Most of the work for this position will be done in the evenings, which will provide me with hours during the day I need to run my business. As well as be available to continue my community service work, speaking in addition to consulting opportunities. Based on my contacts, I was able to submit three business proposals to potential clients. One has replied back with interest in addition to setting up an appointment with me for next week.

Even though I have been successful at landing a rewarding and promising position that will provide opportunities for advancement, I continue to contribute heavily towards my company. The position I have taken provides me with the opportunity to work in an educational setting while building the best practices for leadership and management scholars.

This affords me the ability to continue to work on an additional aspect of my life that I am passionate about, helping individuals to become their best self-possible. I am excited to be professionally free and able to make these choices.

My strategy is very simple and helps to reduce the stress I see many going through layoffs, job loss, or looking for employment experience. I chose to divide my actions into daily manageable activities. In closing, I leave one area of my passion that of Institutional Trust and Financial Markets business to that of educating and building the future of our country in a way which will produce a more positive workforce, those who are engaged and motivated through every step of their career choices, goals, and plans.

Day 31:

I awakened with political capital on my mind. Since I understand the correlation between political capital and career success this is relevant to me. Political capital is a form of influence. In accepting my new role it is important for me to go into the organization by building the proper connections with the right individuals. Influence can halt or slow my ability to move ahead. I am going into both of my roles surrounding myself with the right resources. Therefore what actions I must accomplish?

***PFTIPS*______**

- Ensure that you have established an executive sponsor with cloth in the organization with the first 60 days of your new job.
- Listen carefully before speaking. Many times we miss opportunities because we are too busy talking
- Find out what is important to the executive leadership.
- Understand the culture of the new organization.
- Build partnerships with the right people. This takes careful observation.
- Dress for success, as if you are preparing for the next two positions up.
- Even if allowed to dress casual, find business outfit that can easily go both ways.

- Understand your goals and surround yourself with the resources needed to achieve them.

PROFESSIONAL FREEDOM TRANSITION CHECKLIST

The following is a career transition worksheet. Complete to see if you are prepared for a transition. After completion email me at Marilyn@drmarilyncarroll.com with a copy of your assessment to see if you are ready.

Professional Freedom Career Transition Checklist

This questionnaire has 32 statements. Answer honestly and spontaneously. It should take you only 4-5 minutes to complete.

Please complete the entire questionnaire.

1	Do you understand what direction you would like take your career?	Yes	No
2	Do you know a lot of people who are well connected?	Yes	No
3	Do you have the knowledge, skills and abilities required to be an expert at something you are passionate about?	Yes	No
4	Do you know yourself?	Yes	No
5	Is there a market for your talents and the packaging you have to offer?	Yes	No
6	Are you capable of influencing others by reaching company and/or personal goals?	Yes	No
7	Have you evaluated what your interests are and determined what it is that you like to do?	Yes	No
8	Do you have a solid social network?	Yes	No
9	Do you understand the job requirements and importance of certifications and credentials for your chosen career area of focus?	Yes	No
10	Do certain words come to mind when people think of you?	Yes	No
11	Are pay and benefits important to you?	Yes	No
12	Do you excel in your networking ability?	Yes	No
13	Are you considering a path because you feel that it is safe?	Yes	No
14	Do you understand the importance of social media, especially LinkedIn and the personal info and references/referrals?	Yes	No
15	Are your skills and knowledge up to date and on par with the requirements?	Yes	No
16	Are you hopeful about the future?	Yes	No

17	All else equal, is money a determining factor in your career transition decision?	Yes	No
18	When interacting with others, do you demonstrate apparent sincerity?	Yes	No
19	Have you thought about experiences you have enjoyed?	Yes	No
20	Are you aware of sites like Use LinkedIn/Monster etc	Yes	No
21	Are you technology savvy? Do you use tools such as smart phones, Tablets and other devices frequently?	Yes	No
22	Are you optimistic about moving into your next step in your career?	Yes	No
23	Are you over valued? Can you survive off of less?	Yes	No
24	Are you able to influence others interpersonally?	Yes	No
25	Can you name 5 activities you have enjoyed doing in the past four years?	Yes	No
26	Do you have the name a good employment recruiter?	Yes	No
27	Are you diverse in working between individuals, situations, systems?	Yes	No
28	Can you bounce back from uncertainty? And can you cope with failure?	Yes	No
29	If there is a market for your talent outside of your current location, are you willing to relocate?	Yes	No
30	Are socially astute?	Yes	No
31	Do you have an up-to-date resume?	Yes	No
32	Do you know what you value the most in a job?	Yes	No

Total Number of Yes/Total Number of No's		

BRINGING IT ALL TOGETHER

The nature of work is changing dramatically. The new paradigm consists of ongoing corporate downsizing; technological advances, a global economy, and a growing new independent workforce all represent changes in the work experience for many people. The foundational components of Professional Freedom can help the employment community better prepare for the shift from dependent to independent workforce. Professional Freedom can help with the challenges confronting workers by building interventions to adequately address the new world of employability.

Based on research, individuals with more abundant levels of the individual 12 components of Professional Freedom have more opportunities to be employed than those with less Professional Freedom characteristics. They earn more, have considerable success outcomes in the areas of compensation, career advancement, career mobility, job promotions, life and career satisfaction, connections and political influence. They represent a unique group of individuals who are resilient and can bounce back from adversity and moved on to higher stakes with their career. They have a healthy balance of all the 12 components of Professional Freedom.

They feel secure that they have the proper sustainable balance of a combination of intellectual, social, political, and psychological capital combined with relevant talent, brand awareness, social responsibility, and financial stability to master current and future economic environments associated with employment market conditions. They are competent that they can command market base prices for the services they provide. They can easily shift from one type of business to another and easily apply their talent portfolio offerings to increase or maintain income. They define success based on their terms and strive to master healthy levels of that success for maximum satisfaction and engagement. Each understanding that in order to be a sustainable talent, you must constantly reinvent and re-educate yourself. There are aware of how to adapt and build their career based on their value system. They know when to exit from their current career track and when to take on new directions.

Like many in the career market I had no intentions of staying beyond five years in my previous position. However like many others my first priority was to raise my children. While doing so for many we start to become complacent and then life starts to take the shape of the past need becoming our current circumstance. I was very successful in the financial service industry. I did more than make a living. I built a life for my family which allowed me to stay close to my value system.

The opportunities at previous employers, combined with additional education, helped me to see how my passion for helping others combined with the business knowledge I had gained could be packaged to produce something powerful. The thought of teaching others would not have occurred to me prior to using it as a way to repay my college debt. Teaching is a natural for me. The best opportunities are the ones that you wait and prepare for. My loss has actually been the best thing that's happened to me because I was prepared for it. There are no mistakes in life just opportunities.

Assessing your skills and abilities are important, both personally and professionally. Career management is something that has been on the rise since the mid-eighties. You have to be able to know where you are, where you are headed and you have to be able to gather the resources needed to achieve your goals. It takes more than having the necessary educational knowledge to achieve career success and sustainability, it takes knowledge of "who you are," "who you know," "what you know," "how you know them," and actionable targeted goals to achieve what most think is unachievable. However in order to master it all you must have the right balance of time management skills.

In closing, one area I did not mention in this book was communication skills this includes verbal, written, facial and bodily. Without them you can't adequately get through the twelve components, therefore it is imperative that you understand how to communicate with others in order to gain access to the right networks and forces which help you gain the foundational capital components found in Professional Freedom.

Professional Freedom

I am free and happy because I know who I am and I understand the big picture.

I understand the quality of life I want and seek.

I have a value system which allows me to stay within my ethical boundaries.

I am free and happy because I am prepared for the world of opportunities presented before me and I know what my profession means to me and I to it; remaining knowledgeable about what makes my craft work.

I understand how to build what I seek, my foundation is strong, my connections are getting stronger, and my giving is strong.

The use of my talents is displayed in everything I do.

My image is strong and my ability to connect with others to achieve a common goal is stronger.

My vision of the future strengthens me and those around me.

My ability to dream, understand, achieve, build, rebuild, and test the waters time after time have lead me to an eye, mind and heart for the big picture.

I am free and happy because I understand and have positioned myself to play a starting role in the big picture.

I move each day towards self-actualization through paths of behaviors and the wealth of knowledge I now have within me.

I am free and happy because each day I awake to a world encompassing the right feelings, emotions, allure and satisfaction I receive in knowing that I am professionally free.

This is me!

ABOUT THE AUTHOR

Dr. Marilyn Carroll, Entrepreneur, Professor, Author, and Speaker Dr. Carroll (Marilyn@drmarilyncarroll.com)is the founder and CEO of KSAP5i, Inc., A Career Management Education Company . The company is located in Atlanta, GA, (404)375-8487.

Websites: www.drmarilyncarroll.com or www.ksap5i.com.

Dr. Carroll is responsible for developing and overseeing 21st century career management tools, educational programs and resources for both institutional and retail clients. She has a Ph.D. in Management and Organization with a Leadership Specialization. She is a visiting Professor to several Business Schools lecturing on the following topics: Career and Business Strategies, Leadership, Management, as well as Organizational Behavior and Development. Dr. Carroll has over 20 year's management, coaching, and education experience. She is the mother of two and an active community leader.

Dr. Carroll is passionate about helping others manage their careers. She has spent an extensive amount of time researching career management methodology. She recently launched a series of programs based on career management best practices for success. She has worked with over 1,000 clients using many of the same practices.

REFERENCES

Adams, V.H., Snyder, C.R., Rand, K.L., King, E. A., Sigman, D.R., & Pulvers, K. M. (2002).Hope in the workplace. In R. Giacolone & C. Jurkiewicz (Eds.), *Workplace spiritually and organizational performance*. New York: Sharpe.

Babin, B. J., & Boles, J. S. (1996). The effects of perceived co-worker involvement and supervision support on service provider role stress, performance, and job satisfaction. *Journal of Retailing*, *72*. 57-75.

Babin, B. J., & Boles, J. S. (1998). Employee behavior in a service environment: A model and test of potential differences between men and women. *Journal of Marketing*. *62*. 77-91.

Bakker, A. B., & Demerouti, E. (2007). The job demands-resources model: State of the art. *Journal of Managerial Psychology*, *22*, 309-328.

Barney, J. (1991). Firm Resources and Sustained Competitive Advantage. *Journal of Management Review*, *17*, 99-120.

Bass, B. M.(Ed.). (1985). *Leadership and performance beyond expectation*. New York: Free Press.

Beck, T., Levine, R., & Loayza, N. (2000). Finance and the Sources of Growth. *Journal of Financial Economics, 58*(1-2): 261-300.

Benkoff, B. (1997). Ignoring commitment is costly: New approaches establish the missing link between commitment and performance. *Human Relations*, *50*(6): 701-726.

Bryant, F. B., & Cvengros, J. A. (2004). Distinguishing hope and optimism. *Journal of Applied Psychology*, *23*, 273-302.

Cameron, K. (2008). *Positive leadership strategies for extraordinary performance*. San Francisco: Berrett-Koehler.

Cameron, K., Dutton, J., & Quinn, R. (Eds.). (2003). *Positive organizational scholarship*. San Francisco: Berrett-Koehler.

Carifio, J., & Rhodes, L. (2002). Construct validities and the empirical relationships between optimism, hope, self-efficacy, and locus of control. *Work*, *19*, 125-136.

Connor, D. (1993). *Managing at the speed of change: How resilient managers succeed and prosper where others fail.* New York: Villard Books.

Deming, W. E. (1986). Out of Crisis, MIT Center for Advanced Engineering Study, Cambrige, MA. Retrieved October 15, 2008, from ABI /INFORM Global database.

Drucker, P. F. (Ed.). (1980). *Managing in turbulent times.* New York: Harper & Row.

Evans, M. G. (1970). The effects of supervisory behavior on the path-goal relationship. *Organizational Behavior and Human Performances, 5* 277-298. Retrieved October 15, 2008, from ABI /INFORM Global database.

Flach, F. (1988). *Resilience: Discovering new strength at times of stress.* New York: Facwcett Ballantine.

Frankl, V. (1984). *Man's search for meaning* (3rd ed.). New York: Simon and Schuster, Inc.

Fredrickson, B. L. (1998). What are positive emotions? *Review of General Psychology*, *2*(3), 300-319. Retrieved October 1, 2008, from ABI /INFORM Global database.

Fredickson, B. L. (2001b). The role of positive emotions in positive psychology: The broaden-and-build theory of positive emotions. *American Psychologist. 56* 313-332. Retrieved October 1, 2008, from ABI /INFORM Global database.

Fredrickson, B. L.,Tugade, M. M., Waugh, C. E., & Larkin, G. (2003). What good are positive emotions in crises? *Journal of Personality and Social Psychology*, *84*, 365-376. Retrieved October 1, 2008, from ABI /INFORM Global database.

George, J. M. (1990). Personality, affect, and behaviors in groups. *Journal of Applied Psychology, 75*, 107-116. Retrieved October 1, 2008, from ABI /INFORM Global database.

Gardner, W. L., Avolio, B. J., Luthans, F., May, D. R., & Walumbwa, M. F. (2005). "Can You See the Real Me? A Self-Based Model of Authentic Leader and Follower Development," *The Leadership*

Quarterly, 343-372. Retrieved October 2, 2008, from ABI /INFORM Global database.

Herzberg, F. (1966). *Work and the nature of man.* Cleveland, OH: World

Hobfoll, S. E., Johnson, R. J., Ennis, N. & Jackson, A. P. (2003). Resources loss, resources gain, and emotional outcomes among inner city women. *Journal of Personality and Social Psychology, 84*, 632-643.

James, L. R. and McIntyre, M. D. (1996). Perceptions of organizational climate in Murphy, K. R. (Ed.), *Individual Differences and Behavior in Organizations,* San Francisco: Jossey-Bass.

Jensen, S. M. (2003). *Entrepreneurs as leaders: Impact of psychological capital and perceptions of authenticity on venture performance.* Doctoral dissertation, The University of Nebraska, 3102568).

Jensen, S., Luthans, K., Lebsack, S., & Lebsack, R. (2007). Optimism and employee performance in the banking industry. *The Journal of Applied Management and Entrepreneurship, 12*(3), 57-72.

Jones, E., Kantak, D. M., Futrell, C. M., & Johnston, M. W. (1996). Leader behavior, work attitudes, and turnover of salespeople: An integrative study. *The Journal of Personal Selling and Sales Management, 16(2)*, 13-22.

Judge, T. A., Vianen, A. E. M., & DePater, I. (2004). Emotional stability, core self-evaluations, job outcomes: A review of the evidence and an agenda for future research. *Human Performance, 17*, 325-346.

Kaufman, G. C., & Seelig, S. A. (2002). Post-resolution treatment of depositors at failed banks. *Economic Perspectives* (2nd). Chicago: Federal Reserve Bank of Chicago, (pp. 27-41).

Kernis, M. H. (2003). Toward a conceptualization of optimal self-esteem. *Psychology Inquiry, 14*, 1-26.

Kilburg, R. R. (2001). Facilitating intervention buy-in in executive coaching: A model and methods. *Consulting Psychology Journal: Practice & Research*, 53*(4),* 251-67.

Kirkpatrick, S. A., & Locke, E. A. (1996). Direct and indirect effects of three core charismatic leadership components on performance and attitudes. *Journal of Applied Psychology, 81(1)*, 36-51.

Larson, M. D. (2004). *Positive psychological capital: A comparison with human and social capital and an analysis of a training intervention.* Doctoral dissertation, The University of Nebraska, UMI 3142090).

Leedy, P. D., & Ormrod, J. E. (2005). *Practical research, planning, and design.* New Jersey: Pearson Merrill Prentice Hall.

Lord, R. G., DeVader, C. L., & Alliger, G. M., (1986). A meta-analysis of the relation between personality traits and leadership perceptions: An application of validity generalization procedures. *Journal of Applied Psychology, 71*, 402-410.

Loveman, G. W. (1998). Employee satisfaction, customer loyalty and financial performance: An empirical examination of the service profit chain in retail banking. *Journal of Service Research*, **1**, 18-31.

Luthans, F. (2002a). The need and meaning for positive organizational behavior. *Journal of Organizational Behavior, 23* (6), 695-700.

Luthans, F. (2002b). Positive organizational behavior: Developing and managing psychological strengths. *Academy of Management Executive, 16*, 57-72.

Luthans, F., & Avolio, B. (2003). Authentic leadership: A positive development approach. In Cameron, K. S., Dutton, J. E., & Quinn, R. E. (Eds.). *Positive organizational scholarship,* (pp. 241-258). San Francisco: Berrett-Koehler.

Luthans, F., Avolio, B. J., Avey, J. B., & Norman, S. M. (2007). Positive psychological capital: Measurement and relationship with performance and satisfaction. *Personnel Psychology*, *60*, 541-572.

Luthans, F., Avolio, B. J., Walumbwa, F. O., & Li, W. (2005). The psychological capital of Chinese workers: Exploring the relationship with performance. *Management and Organization Review*, *1*, 249-271.

Luthans, F., Avolio, B. J., & Yousseff, C. (2007). *Psychological Capital: Developing the human capital edge.* Oxford, England: Oxford, University Press.

Luthans, F., Norman, S. M., Avolio, B. J., & Avey, J. B. (2008). The mediating role of psychological capital in the supportive organizational climate: Employee performance relationship. *Journal of Organizational Behavior, 29,* 219-238.

Luthans, F., & Youssef, C. (2004). Human, social and now positive psychological capital management: Investing in people for competitive advantage. *Organizational Dynamics,* **33**, 23-45.

Luthans, F., & Youssef, C. (2007). Emerging positive organizational behavior. *Journal of Management,* 33, 321-349.

Luthans, F., Yousseff, C., & Avolio, B. J (2007).Investing and developing positive organizational behavior. The emergence of psychological capital. In Cooper, C.L., & Nelson, D. (eds.) *Positive organizational behavior: Accentuating the positive at work.* Thousand Oaks, CA: Sage.

Magaletta, P. R., & Oliver, J. M. (1999). The hope construct, will, and ways: Their relations with efficacy, optimism, and general well-being. *Journal of Clinical Psychology*, 55(5), 539-551.

Martin, A. J. (2005). The role of positive psychology in enhancing satisfaction, motivation and productivity in the workplace. *Journal of Organization Behavior Management*, *24*(12), 112-131.

Markus, H., & Wurf, E. (1987). The Dynamic Self-Concept: A Social Psychological Perspective. *Annual Review of Psychology, 38*, 299-337. Retrieved October 1, 2008, from ABI /INFORM Global database.

Maslow, A. (Ed.). (1954). *Motivation and personality*. New York: Harper & Row.

Mastern, A. S. (2001). Ordinary magic: Resilience process in development. *American Psychologist,* 56, 227-239.

McGregor, D. (1960). *The human side of enterprise.* New York: McGraw-Hill.

Norman, S. M. (2006). *The role of trust: Implications for psychological capital and authentic leadership.* (Doctoral dissertation, The University of Nebraska, UMI 3208085).

Parker, S. (1998). Enhancing role breadth self-efficacy: The roles of job enrichment and other organizational interventions. *Journal of Applied Psychology, 6*, 835-852.

Peters, T. & Waterman, R. H. (1982). In Search of Excellence. Lessons from America's Best-run Companies, New York: HarpersCollins Business.

Peterson, C. (2000). The future of optimism. *American Psychologist, 55*, 44-55.

Peterson, S. J., & Luthans, F. (2003). The positive impact and development of hopeful leaders. *Leadership and Organization Development Journal, 24(1),* 26-31.

Pfeffer, J. (1998). *The Human Equation.* Boston: Harvard Business School Press.

Schaufeli, W. B., & Salanova, M. (2007). Work engagement: An emerging psychological concept and its implications for organizations. In Gilliland, S.W., Steiner, D. D., & Skarlicki, D. P. (Eds.). *Research in Social Issues in Management: Managing Social and Ethical Issues in Organizations* (5th ed.). Greenwich, CT: Information Age Publishers.

Scheier, M. F., & Carver, C. S. (1992). Effects of optimism of psychological and physical well-being: Theoretical overview and empirical update. *Cognitive Therapy and Research, 16*, 201-228.

Seligman, M. (1998a). *Learned optimism.* New York: Pocket Books.

Seligman, M. (1998b). Positive social science. *APA Monitor, 29*(2), 5.

Seligman, M. (2002). *Authentic happiness.* New York: Free Press.

Seligman, M., & Csikszentmihalyi, M. (2000). Positive psychology. *American Psychologist, 55,* 5-14.

Sirkin, H. L., Keenan, P., & Jackson, A. (Eds.). (2000). *The Hard Side of Change Management: Harvard Business Review on Leading Through Change.* Boston: Harvard Business Press.

Snyder, C. (1994). Hope and optimism. *Encyclopedia of human behavior* (Vol. 2) (pp. 535-542). Academic Press.

Snyder, C. (1995). Conceptualizing, measuring, and nurturing hope. *Journal of Counseling and Development, 73*, 355-360.

Snyder, C. (2000). *Handbook of hope.* San Diego, CA: Academic Press.

Snyder, C., Harris, C., Anderson, J. R., Holleran, S. A., Irving, L. M., Sigmon, S. T., Yoshinobu, L., et al. (1991). The will and the ways. *Journal of Personality and Social Psychology, 60*. 570-585.

Snyder, C. R., Sympson, S. C., Ybasco, F. C., Borders, T. F., Babyak, M. A., & Higgins, R. L., (1996). Development and validation of the state hope scale. *Journal of Personality and Social Psychology, 70*, 321-335.

Stajkovic, A. D., & Luthans, F. (1998a). Self-efficacy and work-related performance: A meta-analysis. *Psychological Bulletin, 124*. 240-261.

Vroom, V. H. (1964). *Work and motivation.* New York: John Wiley & Sons.

Vugt, V., Hogan, R., & Kaiser, R. B. (2008). Leadership, followership, and evolution.
Some lessons from the past. *American Psychologist, 63*, 182-196.

Waterman, R., Waterman, J., & Collard, B. (1994). Toward a career-resilient workforce. *Harvard Business Review, 72*(4), 87-95. Retrieved March 3, 2008, from ABI /INFORM Global database.

Youssef, C. M. (2004) *Resiliency development of organizations, leaders and employees: Multi-level theory building and individual-level, path-analytical empirical testing.* Doctoral dissertation. The University of Nebraska, AAT 3131572).